DR. TOM MALONE

PREACHES ON

THE CHURCH

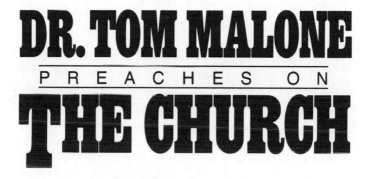

DR. TOM MALONE
P R E A C H E S O N
THE CHURCH

SWORD of the LORD
PUBLISHERS
P.O. BOX 1099, MURFREESBORO, TN 37133

Introduction

I have made little effort toward rigid editing of these sermons. They appear in written form about as they were given in oral form at Emmanuel Baptist Church, Pontiac, Michigan. Neither have I striven to write a theological treatise on the "ekklesia," the "called-out assembly," but have earnestly tried to relate to my congregation what the Bible teaches about THE CHURCH.

I have not written as a theologian, but as a preacher of the Bible on a very vital subject. Not merely have I taught on THE CHURCH, but I have preached these messages in an evangelistic manner, and people were saved, baptized and joined the church during their delivery. I have not preached or written for preachers primarily, but for the people of the pew.

I am convinced of the great emphasis that God places upon the local church and its ministry. It is His own instrument with which He designs to evangelize the world.

"Christ also loved the church, and gave himself for it."— Ephesians 5:25.

Dr. Tom Malone, Sr.

Table of Contents

Chapter I

The Foundation of the Church

Matthew 16:13-19   Matthew 18:15-19

This will be a series of messages from the Bible on "The Church." In Ephesians 5:25 the Word of God says that "Christ also loved the church and gave himself for it." So when talking about the church, we are talking about something Jesus loved enough to give Himself to die for.

The Bible says in James 4:13: "Go to now, ye that say, To day or to morrow we will go into such a city, and continue there a year, and buy and sell, and get gain." The Bible goes on to say that we should say, "If the Lord will, we shall live, and do this, or that." I cannot help but think that there may not be another Wednesday night, there may not be another Lord's day. The Lord Jesus Christ could come at any time. He could come tonight. I believe the stage is set for the coming of the Lord whenever God wills it so. If the Lord tarries, we are going to spend a few weeks studying from the Word of God 113 verses, in the New Testament especially, that deal with the doctrine of the church.

I am going to speak to you one night on "the Symbols of the Church." You see, the Lord has called the church a bride, a body, a building, and so forth.

We will take at least two Wednesday nights speaking on some of the great individual, local churches set forth in the New Testament.

I want to speak one night on "The Organization of the Church." A pattern for the organization of the local New Testament church is set forth explicitly in the Bible.

I want to speak at least two nights on "The Officers of the Church," involving the pastors, bishops, or elders as they are called in the Bible. That involves the board of deacons.

Two nights we will talk on "The Ordinances of the Church." Why do we baptize by immersion only after a person has been genuinely saved? Why do we observe the ordinance of the Lord's Supper? The ordinances of the church, what do they mean?

I will speak one Wednesday on "The Stewardship of the Church." There is much said in the New Testament about the stewardship of the New Testament church.

I will speak one night on "The Orders to the Church of Jesus Christ"—not the ordinances, but the orders.

The final message will be on "The Destiny of the Church." Where will the church ultimately wind up and spend eternity?

I. WHEN DID THE CHURCH BEGIN?

Tonight prayerfully consider with me the subject I have called "The Foundation of the Church of Jesus Christ," or "The Founding of the Church of Jesus Christ." I will read two passages of Scripture in the Book of Matthew as a starting and ending place.

There are various laws of Bible study. One is called the law of prime mention. When is the first time a matter is mentioned in the Bible? Begin where the Bible begins. So I read tonight the first two times "church" is used in the New Testament. The word "church" is never found as such in the Old Testament. We are observing tonight the law of prime mention, when we start with these two passages of Scripture. I am referring to Matthew 16, then Matthew 18.

Look carefully and prayerfully at the reading of the Word of God. I have studied and read it and preached it many times over the years, but I am looking forward for God to bless my own heart through the ministry of the Word. When I am through preaching on these subjects about the church, I want to love the church more. I want to understand more what it means to be a part of it. It is not just an organization, but an organism. We are talking to you tonight about something that lives. The church is alive. It is an organism. It is attached to Jesus Christ as the Head. The church is a living body.

Matthew 16:13-19:

"When Jesus came into the coasts of Caesarea Philippi, he asked his disciples, saying, Whom do men say that I the Son of man am? And they said, Some say that thou art John the Baptist: some, Elias; and others, Jeremias, or one of the prophets. He saith unto them, But whom say ye that I am? And Simon Peter answered and said, Thou art the Christ, the Son of the living God. And Jesus answered and said unto him, Blessed art thou, Simon Bar-jona; for flesh and blood hath not revealed it unto thee, but my Father which is in heaven. And I say also unto thee, That thou art Peter, and upon this rock I WILL BUILD MY CHURCH; and the gates of hell shall not prevail against it. And I will give unto thee the keys of the kingdom of heaven: and whatsoever thou shalt bind on earth shall be bound in heaven: and whatsoever thou shalt loose on earth shall be loosed in heaven."

In Matthew 18:15-19 is the second occurrence of the word "church" in the New Testament. As I say, some 113 times "church" is in the English translation of the Bible.

"Moreover if thy brother shall trespass against thee, go and

*tell him his fault between thee and him alone: if he shall hear thee,
thou hast gained thy brother. But if he will not hear thee, then
take with thee one or two more, that in the mouth of two or three
witnesses every word may be established. And if he shall neglect
to hear them, tell it unto the church: but if he neglect to hear the
church, let him be unto thee as an heathen man and a publican.
Verily I say unto you, Whatsoever ye shall bind on earth shall be
bound in heaven: and whatsoever ye shall loose on earth shall
be loosed in heaven. Again I say unto you, That if two of you shall
agree on earth as touching any thing that they shall ask, it shall
be done for them of my Father which is in heaven."*

What is the Bible saying when the Lord Jesus Christ said to Peter
and the disciples or apostles, "Whatsoever you shall bind on earth
shall be bound in heaven: and whatsoever you shall loose on earth
shall be loosed in heaven"? Matthew 18:19 again: "Again I say
unto you, That if two of you shall agree on earth as touching any
thing that they shall ask, it shall be done for them of my Father
which is in heaven."

Look at two expressions. One in Matthew 16:18: "Upon this
rock I WILL BUILD MY CHURCH." In Matthew 18:17 He said,
'If a brother you are exhorting neglect to hear you, TELL IT TO
THE CHURCH.' These are the first two occurrences of the word
"church" that are actually found in the Bible, occurring for the
first time in the New Testament.

There is a word in the Old Testament that is almost synonymous
with the word "church." There was no such thing as a church
as you and I know it in the Old Testament, a church with ordinances, officers, a Great Commission and all the things that are
in the local church. There are some Old Testament figures or types
of the church such as: Eve, the bride of Adam; and Sarah, the
bride of Abraham; and Rebekah, the bride of Isaac. The Old Testament teaching is primarily not on the church.

I said there is a Hebrew word in the Old Testament which occurs scores of times. If you spell it out in the English, it is *qahal*. That word means "a congregation" and is found approximately one hundred times in the Old Testament. It could be any kind of a congregation. It could be a congregation of angels, a congregation of wicked men, etc. The word also in the Old Testament means "company," "a company of people." It also means "assembly." But the word "church" or the church as we know it tonight is not set forth and revealed in the Old Testament.

Someone comes along and says, "Now wait a minute. Have you read Stephen's sermon in Acts 7?" When he gives a resumé of the history of the children of Israel Stephen says a strange thing about the church. Verse 38 is talking about Moses, the leader of a company in the wilderness in the Old Testament. Stephen says, "This is he, that was in the church in the wilderness with the angel which spake to him in the Mount Sina." There Stephen explicitly mentioned the church in the wilderness, but it merely means what that Hebrew word means—an assembly, a congregation that had been called out. There is no such thing in the Old Testament as a church as you and I know it tonight. If you doubt that, turn to the third chapter of the Ephesians. Ephesians is a beautiful church letter. You will see there that in Old Testament times the truth of the church was hidden from the eyes of Bible believers and friends of God.

Ephesians 3:1-3:

"For this cause I Paul, the prisoner of Jesus Christ for you Gentiles, If ye have heard of the dispensation of the grace of God which is given me to you-ward: How that by revelation he made known unto me the mystery; (as I wrote afore in few words...."

Mystery in the Bible is not something you cannot understand but something hitherto unrevealed.

Ephesians 3:4-9:

*"Whereby, when ye read, ye may understand my knowledge in
the mystery of Christ) WHICH IN OTHER AGES WAS NOT MADE
KNOWN UNTO THE SONS OF MEN, AS IT IS NOW REVEALED
unto his holy apostles and prophets by the Spirit; That the Gentiles should be fellowheirs, and of the same body, and partakers
of his promise in Christ by the gospel: Whereof I was made a
minister, according to the gift of the grace of God given unto me
by the effectual working of his power. Unto me, who am less than
the least of all saints, is this grace given, that I should preach
among the Gentiles the unsearchable riches of Christ; And to make
all men see what is the fellowship of the mystery, WHICH FROM
THE BEGINNING OF THE WORLD HATH BEEN HID IN GOD,
who created all things by Jesus Christ."*

Of course, there is the church in the New Testament. I do not
want to be technical. I want to make it as simple as I possibly
can. There is a word for "church" in the New Testament, *ec-
clesia,* used 113 times. It is a word from which we get "ec-
clesiastic" or "ecclesiastical" or "Ecclesiastes." That word means
"a called-out assembly." The definition of the church of our Lord,
this church, this body, this part of the Bride, this people of God
is "a called-out assembly." That word is developed in the New
Testament, as we will see in the next few weeks, until we have
the New Testament church as you and I know it.

When did the church begin? Some people say, "It began with
Adam. Adam and Eve were both saved by blood." Jesus said later,
"Where two or three are gathered together in my name, there am
I in the midst of them." Some folks say, "There are two believers
saved by blood and the Lord was with them. That's the beginning
of the church."

That is not true. If you will read in Christian literature, you would
find that some people say the church began with Abraham. God
called Abraham out. He said, "Get thee out of thy country and

from thy kindred.'' Finally his household was a constituted, called-out assembly. Some people say that the church began with Abraham.

That is not true. The reason it is not true is because in these instances, and in others as we will see tonight, there were no ordinances, no officers, no commission, no orders. So, these suppositions are not true.

Some folks say the church started with John the Baptist or John the Baptizer. I do not think that is true. I will develop the reason in a moment. There were no ordinances, there was an ordinance of baptism. It is called John's baptism. There were no officers in John's day. There were no deacons. There were no people designated as bishops or pastors as they later were in the Bible. There was no commission, ''Go ye into all the world and preach the gospel to every creature. . .,'' in John's day. So I do not think you can say the church began with John the Baptist.

You may be sitting there tonight saying, ''Well, it doesn't make that much difference when it began. I just know it started.'' I said the same thing myself. I have heard preachers argue over when the church got started. I thought, ''What difference does it make? I'm interested in where it is going to wind up.''

Some people say, ''The church started with Christ on earth.'' Let us see if the Bible says the church started with Christ. In a sense, you will have to say that is true. He did start it. I am talking about the church such as the one sitting in this room right now with all of the components and with all of the ordinances, offices and so forth. Some folks say that it started with Christ at the call of the twelve.

Mark 3 gives the record of the Lord calling twelve people unto Himself. Now these twelve people were all saved except one, who pretended to be. Everybody but Jesus thought him to be. These twelve were all baptized. Some folks say that when Jesus called the twelve the church started. They say, "It had a head." It did. Jesus was right there. They say, "There was a body." There was a body, a body of twelve (eleven specifically). They say, "There was an officer." There was one, but an officer is not demanded in the New Testament teaching about the church. It is good to have one, but it is not explicitly laid out in the Bible that you have that particular officer who was in the twelve, in the Apostolate. Judas was a treasurer. We have one. But the Bible does not demand one. You need a church treasurer, but the Bible did not demand that as an officer of the church. Only two officers are demanded in the Scriptures—deacon and pastor. The office in the Apostolate was not a requisite for the New Testament church. All of these people were baptized; still we cannot say it was the beginning of the church as we know it.

Some folks say that it started with Christ when the incident took place in Matthew 16, when Peter said, "Thou art the Christ, the Son of the living God," and Jesus said, "Upon this rock I will build my church." I submit to you the words of Jesus were futuristic: "I WILL build my church." When Jesus made that statement, we did not have the church as we have it tonight. We had some components, so to speak, of it; but not the church as we have it tonight. We will go back to that Scripture in a moment.

Others say, "The church started with Jesus at the institution of the Lord's Supper." When the Lord's Supper was instituted in Matthew 26, we do have two ordinances. They had not been designated as such, as the only ordinances of the church at this time. There already was John's baptism. Now the Lord in Matthew 26 institutes the Lord's Supper, one of the two ordinances of the church. Still there is no reason, no teaching to say that the church began at the institution of the Lord's Supper.

Others say, "The church began with Jesus, yes. But it began that first Sunday evening after the resurrection when Jesus appeared in the Upper Room with some of the disciples and breathed on them and said, 'Receive ye the Holy Spirit.' " But again, all of the components of the New Testament church as we see it tonight and as it is set forth in the Bible were not present in the Upper Room that night after the resurrection.

When did the church begin? Let us see: did the church begin at Pentecost? That is what most people feel, what most Baptists, I think, believe.

Let us look at something. The church was apparently future when Jesus said, "Upon this rock I will build my church." Not long after that Jesus died and arose and Pentecost came and all of the components of the church immediately came about. So it was future when Jesus in Matthew 16 said, "I will build my church."

Think for a moment. What is the church founded upon? The Bible tells us that the church is founded upon the death and the resurrection and the ascension of Christ. Until just before Pentecost, Christ had not ascended. You say, "Why do you say that the ascension of Christ was necessary for the beginning of the church?" Well, Jesus intercedes for the church in Heaven. Not only that, but the Bible says that when He ascended on High, He led captivity captive, that is, He moved the saints out of Abraham's bosom and moved them up to Heaven. When He ascended unto Heaven, He led captivity captive and gave gifts unto them. The church functions through gifted people. You cannot possibly say the church began before Pentecost. Ephesians 1:22, 23: "And hath put all things under his feet, and gave him to be the head over all things to the church, Which is his body, the fulness of him that filleth all in all." That could only be possible after His ascension.

Notice something else. When did these Christians become a body? That is what the church is. What officially took place on the day of Pentecost? We have talked to you about the Holy Spirit. We have talked to you about the baptism of the Holy Spirit, something a lot of folks are afraid of. If some wild-eyed religious person came up to you and asked, "Have you been baptized of the Holy Ghost?" it would scare some of them to death! If they ever do, here is how I want you to do it. If someone asks you, "Have you been baptized with the Holy Ghost?" look them right in the eye, smile and say, "I most certainly have." Because you have. It took place on the day of Pentecost and it is only mentioned after the Book of Acts one time in the whole New Testament, in I Corinthians 12:13: "For by one Spirit are we all baptized into one body, whether we be Jews or Gentiles, whether we be bond or free; and have been all made to drink into one Spirit." There was no such thing as a body, speaking of the church, until the day of Pentecost when the baptism of the Holy Ghost took place. So the baptism of the Holy Spirit took place. That is the formulation of individual Christians into one body.

That is a beautiful truth. We are not just lots of people. We are one body. Paul likened it to a physical body: "The hand cannot say to the foot, I have no need of thee. The eye cannot say to the ear, I have no need of thee." He said, "We are individuals, but we are one body." That formally, dispensationally took place on the day of Pentecost.

Let us look at something else, then I will move on. A verse in Ephesians talks about the church. The Book of Ephesians is the beautiful epistle that teaches about the church mystical as well as the church local. It says in Ephesians 2:21: "In whom all the building [that is, the church] fitly framed together groweth unto an holy temple in the Lord." Watch this in the next verse: "In whom ye also are builded together for an habitation of God through the Spirit." That never took place until Pentecost. The Holy Spirit never inhabited believers as He is right tonight in every one of us, until after the day of Pentecost.

The Bible plainly shows that He came and He went. He touched one here and there. But since the day of Pentecost, He indwells every believer. God is not inhoused in this framework of a building you see and touch and feel. But the Holy Spirit is inhoused in this living body right here tonight. That never took place until after the day of Pentecost.

There is a development of teaching after that until we come to what we have here tonight.

II. UPON WHOM IS THE CHURCH FOUNDED?

I want to answer another question before closing. Who is the rock upon which the church is founded or built? You say, "O Preacher, I know that." No you don't. Many don't know who claim to be people of God. They do not know upon whom the church is built. I am not fighting Catholics. I love them and want to see them accept the same Jesus who came into this unsaved Methodist's heart in 1935. You ask a Catholic to explain to you Matthew 16 and he will tell you that Jesus founded the church upon the Apostle Peter. The answer is neither evident nor simple. Millions of people do not believe that the church is founded upon Jesus Christ.

In Matthew 7:24 the Lord used a wonderful illustration. He likens life unto the building of a house. He is talking about the importance of the foundation. He is talking about two foundations. He said a man built a house upon a rock and a man built a house upon the sand. He said that the rain descended and floods came and the winds blew and beat upon the house built upon the sand and it fell. Great was the fall of it. But Jesus said of the house builded upon the rock, the same wind blew and the same floods came and beat upon the house and it fell not, for it was founded upon the rock. No doubt Jesus had reference to that when He said, "Upon this rock I will build my church" (Matt. 16:18).

So let us ascertain that the church is founded, not on a loose stone, but upon a permanent Rock, because that is what the Lord is talking about: "Upon this rock I will build my church, and the gates of hell shall not prevail against it."

Some folks say, "Well, Peter was that rock," getting that from John 1:42 where for the first time Simon Peter was introduced to Jesus Christ by his brother, Andrew. When Jesus beheld him, He said, "Thou art Simon, the son of Jona: thou shalt be called Cephas, which is by interpretation, a stone" (John 1:42). The word for stone there is *petros*. There are two words in the New Testament for the word stone. One is *petros* and the other is *Petra*. *Petros* in the New Testament refers to stone. Someone has said it is like a rolling stone. It is a stone that one could pick up and throw. When Jesus said, "...thou shalt be called Cephas, which is by interpretation, a stone," He used the word *petros* in the New Testament, a small stone, a stone you can pick up, a movable, rolling rock or stone.

When Jesus said, "Upon this rock I will build my church," He was not using the word He used for Peter. He was using the word *Petra* which means a great ledge of rock or a great foundation rock, not one that can be moved, not one that you can throw, not one that can be rolled. It was a permanent stone. That is the word Jesus used when He said, "Upon this rock I will build my church."

Let us listen in on the conversation.

Jesus said, "Whom do men say that I am?"

Peter said, "Thou art the Christ, the Son of the living God."

Jesus said, "Blessed art thou, Simon Bar-jona: for flesh and blood hath not revealed it unto thee. You didn't come to know I was the Son of God by any human means. Flesh and blood [speaking of humanity] did not reveal this unto thee, but my Father which is in heaven. And I say unto thee, That thou art Peter [*petros*], thou art a stone I can pick up. But upon this rock—and you just said I am the Son of God—upon THIS rock I will build my church."

There is not the slightest indication that Jesus said, "I am going to build my church on Simon Peter."

He gave him a name in John 1:42. He promised him that name. He gave it to him here in Matthew 16, then said that upon the great solid rock "I will build my church."

Notice that this is determined in the Bible. In I Corinthians 10:4 we read, "...that Rock was [or is] Christ." There is no doubt upon whom the church is founded. Isaiah prophesied that the church would be built upon a rock: "Therefore thus saith the Lord God, Behold, I lay in Zion for a foundation a stone, a tried stone, a precious corner stone, a sure foundation" (Isa. 28:16). That is why Paul said, "For other foundation can no man lay than that is laid, which is Jesus Christ" (I Cor. 3:11).

I thank God that my church of which I am a little part is not built upon a rolling stone or a human being, but is founded upon the eternal, permanent Son of God. "Upon THIS ROCK I will build my church."

III. WHAT IS MEANT BY BINDING AND LOOSING?

Following that is the most controversial Scripture in all the Bible. Jesus said to Peter then, "And I will give unto thee the keys of the kingdom of heaven [not the keys of the church]...." Then He said something that is later clarified, that it is given to all of the disciples: "Whatsoever thou shalt bind on earth shall be bound in heaven: and whatsoever thou shalt loose on earth shall be loosed in heaven."

When Jesus said, "I give unto thee the keys of the kingdom of heaven," there are folks who say He gave Peter the right and the ability to forgive sins. That is not what it is talking about. Now a key is to open a door. Peter opened the door twice. He opened it on the day of Pentecost when he preached the truth of the Gospel and said, "Whosoever shall call upon the name of the Lord shall be saved." He opened the door to the Jew in Acts 2. In Acts 10 he went to the house of Cornelius, the Gentile, and used the keys again and opened the door of the Gospel.

When the Bible says, "Whatsoever shall be bound on earth shall be bound in heaven," God is saying that to "bind" is to "prohibit" and to "loose" is to "permit." If something is bound, then it is prohibited. We are bound by law. We are bound by promises. That means we are prohibited to go beyond that. Peter used it just like that. To bind is to prohibit, and to loose means to permit.

Look at the last few verses of Acts 10. It is about Gentiles' being saved. Listen! Don't think this matter of Gentiles' getting saved was an ordinary thing. The Bible says it was to the "Jew first, then also to the Greek [the Gentile]" (Rom. 1:16). Jews did not think any Gentiles would ever get saved. They called them dogs. When Peter was told to go to the house of Cornelius, a Gentile, and preach, he said, "I can't do it. They are unclean." The Lord by illustration showed him that he was called to go to the Gentiles. So he went to the house of Cornelius and preached. They believed and were wonderfully saved. At the close of Acts 10, we read these words:

"And they of the circumcision which believed were astonished, as many as came with Peter, because that on the Gentiles also was poured out the gift of the Holy Ghost. For they heard them speak with tongues [languages], and magnify God. Then answered Peter, Can any man forbid water, that these should not be baptized, which have received the Holy Ghost as well as we?"—Acts 10:45-47.

Peter is saying, "This is loosed in Heaven and loosed on earth. Permit them to be baptized."

Not one thing in the Bible teaches that a man can forgive sin.

When Jesus said to the man let down through the roof, "Rise, take up thy bed and walk," He saved him. When He did, they accused Jesus. "Who can forgive sins, but God only?" (Mark 2:7).

I ask the same question tonight, "Who can forgive sin, but God only?" No man! "For there is one God, and one mediator between God and men, the man Christ Jesus; Who gave himself a ransom for all, to be testified in due time" (I Tim. 2:5, 6). No one but Jesus Christ.

Now then, the way into the church is, you have to be born again. That is the only way. In a sense, you do not really join. That is the visible act that makes you a member of a local church. It is very important. Everybody ought to do it. To get into the body of Christ you have to be born again. You have to be born the second time, then you are a member of His body and a member of it forever. "Jesus answered, Verily, verily, I say unto thee, Except a man be born of water and of the Spirit, he cannot enter into the kingdom of God" (John 3:5).

Chapter II

What Is the Church?

I Corinthians 12:12-31

Last Wednesday night we spoke to you on what we call "The Foundation of the Church." Now tonight I start with, "What Is the Church?" Let us read from the Word of God. We have spoken quite a bit lately from certain verses in I Corinthians 12. It is the only reference in the New Testament after the Book of Acts to what is called the "baptism of the Holy Ghost." We have made reference to that numerous times recently. It is a chapter dealing with what is called the gifts of the Spirit. But I want tonight to see something else we have not touched on at all. We shall begin reading in verse 12 and read to the end of the chapter of I Corinthians 12. You will notice a repetition of one word over and over again in this passage of Scripture, the word "body." One thing the Bible says the church is, is a body. First Corinthians 12:12-31:

"For as the body is one, and hath many members, and all the members of that one body, being many, are one body: so also is Christ. For by one Spirit are we all baptized into one body, [the tense in verse 13 is in the "aorist" tense in the Greek, which is always past tense in this verse. I want us to learn that because the baptism of the Holy Spirit is something that had already taken place on the day of Pentecost] *whether we be Jews or Gentiles, whether we be bond or free; and have been all made to drink into*

one Spirit. For the body is not one member, but many. If the foot shall say, Because I am not the hand, I am not of the body; is it therefore not of the body? If the whole body were an eye, where were the hearing? If the whole were hearing, where were the smelling? But now hath God set the members every one of them in the body, as it hath pleased him. And if they were all one member, where were the body? But now they are many members, yet but one body. And the eye cannot say unto the hand, I have no need of thee: nor again the head to the feet, I have no need of you. Nay, much more those members of the body, which seem to be more feeble, are necessary: [Those members of the body which seem to be more feeble are necessary. This is true of the human body and it is true of the body of Christ.] *And those members of the body, which we think to be less honourable, upon these we bestow more abundant honour; and our uncomely parts have more abundant comeliness. For our comely parts have no need: but God hath tempered the body together, having given more abundant honour to that part which lacked: That there should be no schism* [or division] *in the body; but that the members should have the same care one for another. And whether one member suffer, all the members suffer with it; or one member be honoured, all the members rejoice with it. Now ye are the body of Christ, and members in particular. And God hath set some in the church, first apostles, secondarily prophets, thirdly teachers, after that miracles, then gifts of healings, helps, governments, diversities of tongues. Are all apostles? are all prophets? are all teachers? are all workers of miracles? Have all the gifts of healing? do all speak with tongues? do all interpret? But covet earnestly the best gifts: and yet shew I unto you a more excellent way.''*

That ''excellent way'' is the subject of chapter 13, which is love. We will start tonight with verse 27, ''Now ye are the body of Christ, and members in particular.'' Eighteen times in sixteen verses, from verse 12 down through verse 27, "body" is used as a symbol or type of the church. Mind you: the Bible teaches you and me a great deal in type and in symbol, all through the Bible, beginning from the very first to the very end of the Bible.

The rock in Exodus 17 is called the smitten rock. The Bible says that rock was Christ. So there that smitten rock that gave forth the fountain of water is a picture of the smitten Christ on the cross giving forth the water of life.

In John 1:29 John the Baptist said, "Behold the Lamb of God, which taketh away the sin of the world." When he said "Lamb," he pointed to the Son of man, Jesus Christ. There you have a lamb as a picture or type or symbol of Jesus Christ.

In John 10:11 Jesus said, "I am the good shepherd: the good shepherd giveth his life for the sheep." There you have a shepherd as a symbol or picture or type of the Lord Jesus Christ. The Holy Spirit has chosen to use types and symbols to teach us what He is speaking about. The Bible teaches by types or symbols.

In order to understand what the church is, we have to see the symbols and types that God used in relation to the church.

I. WHAT THE CHURCH IS NOT

I would like to, first, say what the church is not. I know that many think the church is something that it really is not. We read an expression, "the kingdom of heaven," over and over in the New Testament. In fact, Matthew 13 has seven parables Jesus used about the kingdom of Heaven. But the kingdom of Heaven is not the church. The kingdom of Heaven is the earthly sphere of the universal kingdom of God, while the kingdom of God is universal. Jesus used various parables about it. It is not the church.

For instance, in one of these parables Jesus said that a man went out and sowed good seed in his field—Matthew 13:25: "But while men slept, his enemy came and sowed tares among the wheat...."

He is teaching that in the kingdom of Heaven there are both wheat and tares. Tares are unsaved people who imitate saved people.

He went on to say in that same chapter that the kingdom of Heaven is like a net that a man cast into the sea and then drew to shore a great number of fish. Good fish he kept, bad fish he threw away. But in the net there were both good and bad. Such is the kingdom of Heaven. Literally multitudes of church members have never been saved. The kingdom of Heaven has in it real and unreal professors. So the church is not the kingdom of Heaven.

The church is not a building. In the strictest biblical sense, this building in which we have been worshiping the Lord and meeting as a church all these years is not a church. Many people drive along the highway and say, "Oh, there's a church." But they are not seeing a church. Remember Stephen in his sermon in Acts 7 said, "Howbeit the most High dwelleth not in temples made with hands." Remember Paul in Athens, preaching on Mars' Hill, said as he looked at the mighty Acropolis and the great buildings there in Athens, "God dwelleth not in temples made with hands" (Acts 17:24).

This building was made with hands. In fact, these two hands helped build some of it. So this is not the church. The church is not a building. I want you to remember that because, God willing, next week I will speak on "The Church Is Called a Temple." It is a spiritual temple, never a material building.

The church is not the kingdom of Heaven. The church is not a building. And the church is not a denomination. By denomination, I mean a great system of churches with ecclesiastical hierarchy, etc., as we know denominations today.

You may say, "Well, we belong to the Baptist denomination." In a sense we are not a denomination. We have no headquarters on earth. The only tie between this church and any other independent, fundamental Baptist church is the tie of fellowship. There is no other tie between New Testament churches. Fifteen times John, the forerunner of Jesus, was referred to as "John the Baptist." No doubt he was called that because he baptized so many thousands in the Jordan River. From that designation of John— John the Baptist—we have literally thousands of churches around the world which are called Baptist but are not a denomination as such.

You would say, "The Southern Baptist Convention, the American Baptist Association, the United Methodists are denominations." But the church is not a denomination in any sense of the word. There is no teaching in all the Bible to substantiate the matter of organized denominations.

I really should not pass over this. Many think of the church as being an invisible body. They speak of an invisible church. I guess there is such a thing. There are some members of the Lord's church who are in France and Germany, Israel and Australia and all around the world. I have never seen them and never will. I guess there is such a thing as an invisible church. There are many members of the Lord's church who died long before you and I were born, so we never saw them. If the Lord tarries, after you and I are gone, there will be more, thank God, who will be born again into the family of God and will be a part of the church of Jesus Christ. I want you to know that the emphasis in the Word of God is not on an invisible church. The emphasis in the New Testament is on a visible church or a local church. I said that we would start tonight on verse 27 just for that reason.

II. THE CHURCH IS A BODY

This is the Corinthian epistle. It is addressed to the Corinthian church. To the Corinthian church Paul talked about the ordinances: baptism in water and the Lord's Supper. Verse 27: "Now ye are the body of Christ." So that church at Corinth was, according to Paul, the body of Christ. Just as much as the whole human body is one body, so the New Testament local church is the body of Christ.

So, first, let us see tonight that the church is a body, that is, it is an organic whole made up of many members. When we speak of the church as a body and having many members, we are talking about diversity, yet unity.

All of us are not alike. We do not all have the same gift. We do not all minister the same service. We are members of a body, yet there is diversity. We are not all alike but we are in unity because we are one body.

That is why Paul said, "The foot cannot say to the hand, I have no need of thee." When it speaks of an organic whole, it presupposes both diversity and unity. The church is a body. Notice first (we commented on it a moment ago) verse 13: "For by one Spirit are we all baptized into one body...." God is saying we ARE one body. God said, 'If one member suffers, the whole body suffers. If one member is honoured, the whole body is honoured.' Why? Because the church is a unified body. We are not separate. Individuals, yes, but unified in one body, the body of Christ. "For by one Spirit are we all baptized into one body, whether we be Jews or Gentiles, whether we be bond or free; and have been all made to drink into one Spirit."

III. IT IS A BODY WITH A HEAD

Now three things about the church as a body. First, it is a body with a head. God is very careful in His Word to tell us who the head of the church, the head of the body, is. Colossians 1:18 says, "And he [that is, Christ] is the head of the body, the church; who is the beginning, the firstborn from the dead; that in all things he might have the preeminence." The head of the church is Jesus Christ—Ephesians 1:22: "And hath put all things under his feet, and gave him to be the head over all things to the church.''

Head means "chief" or "supreme ruler." In the strictest sense of the word no man is the head of the church. I believe that pastors are looked upon as undershepherds. But the head of the church is Jesus Christ. He is the head of the body, not a pope. The Roman Catholic pope, with millions and millions of constituents and adherents, poses as being the head of the church, Christ's vicar over all.

I do not go around trying to fight Catholic people. There are also a lot of unsaved Baptists. The only way we are going to win them is to love them and give them the truth of the Word of God. So, I am not fighting Catholics. But I want to say to you, there is no such thing as an infallible man. There has never been one who ever walked the face of this earth, but Jesus Christ who said, "I do always those things that please him" (John 8:29). The head of the church is He of whom it was said, "This is my beloved Son, in whom I am well pleased" (Matt. 3:17). The pope is a sinner like Tom Malone. Unless he is saved by the blood of Jesus Christ, he will be as lost as any lost man could ever be and will burn in Hell. I am not saying he is saved or lost. I am saying if he trusts Jesus Christ, he is saved. If he does not, he is lost. I do not know how a man could be saved from sin who never thought he had ever sinned. There is no such thing as an infallible man. The church is not headed up by the pope.

Neither is the church headed up by any organization. Multitudes look to some kind of ecclesiastical hierarchy in their denomination. They have what they call bishops, elders, presidents and headquarters. You do not find that in the Bible. Christ is the head of the church. People ask me, "Where is the headquarters of your church?" They ask, "What directory are you listed in? Where is your home office? Where is the head of your church?" I always tell them, "In Heaven." That settles it. They go away saying,

"He's a nut anyhow. There is no use talking to him." The church is a body with a head.

IV. IT IS A UNIFIED BODY

Second, the church is a body with unity. See the picture tonight. It sounds so simple, yet it is so beautiful, so wonderful, so necessary to understand. The church is a body with unity.

In Romans 12 there is this statement:

"For as we have many members in one body, and all members have not the same office: So we, being many, are one body in Christ, and every one members one of another."—Vss. 4, 5.

We are unified. We have been bonded together spiritually. The body of Christ is a body with unity.

That is why Paul used that expression, "The foot cannot say to the hand, I have no need of thee." We have two feet, a left foot and a right foot. Suppose the left foot says, "I'm going to go north," and the right foot says (it is another member, you see, diversified, yet unified), "I think I'll go south." There would be a division, would there not? That probably would hurt before it was over with! Did you know that both of those members get their direction from the head? The head would never say, "One foot go north, the other go south." The body is a unity. The members are always in touch with the head. It is not only a body with a head, but it is a body with unity.

V. IT IS A FUNCTIONAL BODY

It is a body which is functional. If we brought a corpse in here tonight in a casket and somebody said, "That's a body," he would be exactly right. That body would be dead and have no life in it.

But that is not the kind of body the Lord is talking about for the church. It is a functional body, not a corpse. That is why Paul said in I Corinthians 12:4, "Now there are diversities of gifts, but the same Spirit." It is a functional body.

Two women in the Old Testament are types, in a sense, of the church. One is Eve. God caused a deep sleep to fall on Adam. From Adam's side He took a rib and made a woman. (Dr. Lakin says that a man's rib was the first part God ever used to make a loudspeaker!)

Now look at a very beautiful picture in the Bible of the church. First, a deep sleep upon Adam, a deep sleep likened unto the death of Jesus on the cross. Then God opened Adam's side. On the cross God opened the side of the Son of God. Notice after that God made a new body that had never been in existence before. Adam was created from the direct hand of God. Eve was made when the bleeding side of a man named Adam was opened. A new body was brought forth. Picture the body of Christ, bought by the precious blood of the Son of God. Then what happened? God said that this new body, this new life, and this man out of whose side she was taken "shall be one flesh" (Gen. 2:24). Friend, that is a picture of the closeness of the church to Jesus Christ. We are one in Him. The church is a body, but it is a functional body which serves.

VI. IT IS A BRIDE

Now I go one step further. First, the church is set forth in the New Testament as a body. Second, it is set forth as the Bride. In Revelation 21:9 we read these words: "Come hither, I will shew thee the bride, the Lamb's wife." The church is pictured as a bride of Jesus Christ.

I said two women in the Old Testament are tremendous pictures of the bride of Christ, the church. First, Eve. Now the church is not taught in the Old Testament, but in shadow and symbol and type there is a beginning of the teaching. I refer to this second woman, Rebekah, discussed in Genesis 24. It is like a beautiful love story, a beautiful drama, if you please, with four main characters. There is a father, Abraham; a son, Isaac; an unnamed servant; and a young woman, Rebekah.

You know the story. Abraham sent his trusted servant to a distant land to get a bride for his son, Isaac. God the Father sent His Son from Heaven to a distant land to get a bride. He sent the Holy Spirit to do that. Abraham is a picture of God the Father. Isaac waits contentedly. He has never seen his bride-to-be and she has never seen him. It is a beautiful story. Just before the unnamed servant with the regiment of people comes back and Rebekah is to meet Isaac, Isaac goes out by the well of Lahairoi. What is he doing? Praying, waiting for his bride to come and join him. That is exactly what our Heavenly Isaac is doing. He is at the throne of God to make intercession for us, waiting for His bride to come.

We read of a servant whose name is not given, for the Bible says that the Holy Spirit would not speak of Himself; He would speak of another. Here is an unnamed servant sent by the father who spoke only of the groom whom the young woman was soon to meet.

Here is Rebekah. She loved Isaac before she ever saw him. We have never seen Jesus Christ. No man has seen God at any time—I Peter 1:8: "Whom having not seen, ye love: in whom, though now ye see him not, yet believing, ye rejoice with joy unspeakable and full of glory." Though she had never seen him, Rebekah was willing to make a long journey. You and I, the church, are on a long journey. God calls us pilgrims. We are a traveling group, just passing through. It has always been that way with the church. We are on our way to meet the Groom in the sky.

After a long journey, Rebekah was received into the home of her husband's father. Jesus said, "In my Father's house are many mansions: if it were not so, I would have told you. I go to prepare a place for you. And if I go and prepare a place for you, I will come again" (John 14:2, 3). Isaac is a type of Jesus. Remember, it was Isaac with the wood on his back who climbed Mount Moriah. He was bound and laid upon an altar, willing to die. His father was willing to sacrifice him. Isaac is a picture of Jesus Christ. The mountain was Golgotha, the wood was the cross upon His back. The church is pictured in the Bible as a bride getting ready to meet the groom, her husband.

Now watch something. This bride is adorned and waiting. In speaking of the bride of Isaac, the Bible says, "And the servant brought forth jewels of silver, and jewels of gold, and raiment, and gave them to Rebekah" (Gen. 24:53). Revelation 19:7, 8 says:

"Let us be glad and rejoice, and give honour to him: [to Christ] *for the marriage of the Lamb is come, and his wife hath made herself ready. And to her was granted that she should be arrayed in fine linen, clean and white: for the fine linen is the righteousness of the saints."*

You see, the church is adorned and made beautiful. This bride is adorned and waiting for that glorious, thrilling moment when the bride shall meet the Groom, never to be separated again.

There is a reason why we read that the church is dressed up in fine linen, which is the righteousness of the saints. That is the righteousness of Christ imputed unto every saved person. There is a reason for that. Ephesians 5:27 teaches us that one day the Lord is going to present His bride in Heaven. Here is the way she will be presented: "That he might present it to himself a glorious church, not having spot, or wrinkle, or any such thing; but that it should be holy and without blemish." It is an adorned bride, perfectly clothed in the righteousness of Jesus Christ.

Thank God for the righteousness of Jesus! That is the only reason we could ever be presented without a wrinkle, without a spot and without a blemish. There are no wrinkles in the robe of righteousness, and no spots or stains on it. There is not a single blemish in the righteousness of Christ which we have tonight.

The church is a much-loved bride. It we could realize how much this bride, the church of Jesus, is loved. Ephesians 5:25 says: "Husbands, love your wives, even as Christ also loved the church, and gave himself for it." It is a bride purchased with His own blood.

When this unnamed servant went to get an unseen bride for Isaac, a type of Christ, he took with him gifts. Bracelets were put on her hands and gifts were given unto her from her groom-to-be whom she had never seen.

The Lord Jesus has done the same thing. When you and I were saved, He gave to us what is called an "earnest" or a downpayment, the gift of the Holy Ghost. In every heart, in every body of every saved person, there is this earnest, this guarantee that one day the bride is going to meet this Groom, never to be separated.

The church is a body and a bride.

"In whom ye also trusted, after that ye heard the word of truth, the gospel of your salvation; in whom also after that ye believed, ye were sealed with that holy Spirit of promise, which is the earnest of our inheritance until the redemption of the purchased possession, unto the praise of his glory."—Eph. 1:13, 14.

Chapter III

The Symbols of the Church

This wonderful passage of Scripture will bless the heart of anyone who looks upon this Word of God. In Ephesians 2 we shall begin reading with verse 14 and read to the end of the chapter.

It so happens there are only four symbols of the church that I find in the Bible. By symbol I mean something God used to represent and to make clear the meaning of the church. It so happens that two of them are found in this Scripture we will read tonight. May the Lord please make His Word clear to our hearts.

By the way, Ephesians is the only book in the Bible in which all four of these symbols are mentioned. Remember we dealt with the church as the body of Christ. That is a symbol or a picture of the church, the body. Then we dealt with the church as a bride. All four of these—the body, the bride, the church as a new man and the church as a spiritual temple—are set forth in the Book of Ephesians. Some are mentioned in other books, but no Book mentions all four of these representations of the church except Ephesians, often called "the Church Epistle." Certainly the church is found all through this book of six chapters.

Let us begin reading with verse 14 of Ephesians 2:

"For he is our peace, who hath made both one [talking about the Jew and the Gentile], *and hath broken down the middle wall of partition between us; Having abolished in his flesh the enmity,*

even the law of commandments contained in ordinances; for to make in himself of twain one new man, so making peace; And that he might reconcile both unto God in one body by the cross, having slain the enmity thereby: And came and preached peace to you which were afar off, and to them that were nigh. For through him we both [Jew and Gentile] *have access by one spirit unto the Father. Now therefore ye are no more strangers and foreigners, but fellowcitizens with the saints, and of the household of God; and are built upon the foundation of the apostles and prophets...."*

I want to point out in reading here that we spoke one night on "The Foundation of the Church." It is very plain and clear in the Bible that Jesus is the foundation of the church, though it seems to be suggested in verse 20 that the apostles and prophets are the foundation of the church. It is merely referring to the fact that the apostles and prophets laid down the foundation of the church which is Jesus Christ in their teaching. The church is not built upon the apostles, nor upon prophets but upon Christ. The foundation of the church is Jesus Christ Himself. "For other foundation can no man lay than that is laid, which is Jesus Christ" (I Cor. 3:11). Jesus said, "Upon this rock [His deity, His Person] I will build my church."

Now notice Ephesians 2:19-22:

"Now therefore ye are no more strangers and foreigners, but fellowcitizens with the saints, and of the household of God; And are built upon the foundation of the apostles and prophets, Jesus Christ himself being the chief corner stone; in whom all the building fitly framed together groweth unto an holy temple in the Lord: In whom ye also are builded together for an habitation of God through the Spirit."

Let me review for a moment. We talked to you one night on

"the Church as a Body." In Ephesians 1:23 we read, "...the church, which is his body, the fulness of him that filleth all in all." There is no question that the church is set forth as a body. We also dealt with the subject, "The Church as a Bride." In Ephesians 5:25 we read: "Husbands, love your wives, even as Christ also loved the church, and gave himself for it." In Revelation 21:9 we read, "Come hither, I will shew thee the bride, the Lamb's wife." The church is pictured as a bride and a body.

I. THE CHURCH IS PICTURED AS A NEW MAN

In the Scripture, the church is pictured in two more ways. They are the only four symbols I find in the Bible representing the church. Some say the church is pictured as sheep. That is not true. I know that Jesus said, "I am the good shepherd; the good shepherd giveth his life for his sheep" (John 10:11). But this is talking about an individual believer as a sheep, not as a church. The church is not pictured as a sheep in the Bible.

There are those who even say that the church is pictured as branches, referring to John 15:5 where Jesus said, "I am the vine, ye are the branches." That is not talking about the church; this is talking as individuals. He is the life-giving vine and individuals are looked upon as fruit-bearing branches of all the vine, even the Lord Jesus Christ.

Others go so far as to say that the church is pictured as a soldier in the Bible, especially in the Book of Ephesians, getting that idea from Ephesians 6 where so much is said about the Christian dressing up in the spiritual armor that God has given him. Paul said, "Thou therefore endure hardness, as a good soldier of Jesus Christ" (II Tim. 2:3). But he is not talking about the church as a corporate body; he is talking about individuals.

When we read of a sheep, we are reading of an individual believer. When we read of a branch, that is an individual Chris-

tian. When we read of a soldier, that is an individual Christian.
As a sheep, you follow His voice; as a branch, you bear His fruit;
as a soldier, you fight His cause.

You are a branch. You are a sheep. You are a soldier. But I
could not set any born-again child of God out by himself tonight
and call him a church. A church means more than one individual
believer.

There are only four symbols in the New Testament that represent the church: a BODY, a BRIDE, a NEW MAN, a SPIRITUAL
TEMPLE.

I want us to see those four pictures tonight. I think God wants
to bring these symbols or representations of the church before us
so we can know what the church is. How beautifully the body pictures the church! Not the same office but many members representing the body of Christ.

It is the same with the two symbols. First, the church is pictured as a new man. In Ephesians 4:14 the individual Christian
is told, ''And that ye put on the new man, which after God is
created in righteousness and true holiness.'' That is an individual
Christian. He is a new man. There is no question but that the church
is pictured as a new man. This is the reason. Broadly speaking,
there are in the Bible two great classes of people: the Jew with
whom God dealt first; the Gentile with whom God is dealing in
this age of grace. These were always divided, always separated.
In fact, someone has pointed out that there are five great barriers
between the Jew and the Gentile. There is not a person here tonight
who does not know of the division and, yes, even the racial hatred
that has existed and will continue to exist between the Jew and
the Gentile. The Gentile represents all other nations. There are
five great barriers between the Jew and the Gentile. Thank God,
every one of them has been dissolved in the Scripture that we read
to you tonight.

There is a DISTANCE problem. Chapter 2 talks about lost people: "...ye who sometimes were far off are made nigh by the blood of Christ" (vs. 13). The Jew looked upon himself as being close to God while the Gentile was looked upon as being far off from the Lord. Now the Bible says, "...ye who sometimes were far off [that is, the Gentile] are made nigh by the blood of Christ." So there is a distance problem.

There was the problem of DISUNION. There was no peace between the Jew and the Gentile. God set forth under law certain rules and regulations that Jews were to live by. They could not marry a Gentile since they were really a separate people. There was no peace between them. Here the Scripture says, "For he is our peace, who hath made both one" (vs. 14).

There is no such thing in the church now as Jew and Gentile. It is the church of God made up of blood-washed, saved people. This disunion has been taken care of because God puts peace in the heart of a saved Jew and saved Gentile and makes them one in Christ Jesus. So disunion has been taken care of.

There is the matter of DIVISION. Even the Old Testament Tabernacle, later the Temple, was divided into three divisions. There were two large partitions. One of those made a court. The outer court, the farthest court away from the Holy of Holies, was called the Court of the Gentiles. This Scripture says that He "hath broken down the middle wall of partition between us" (vs. 14). Some think it may refer to the veil which covered the Holy of Holies, rent from the top to the bottom when Jesus died. There is no partition now between saved Jews and saved Gentiles. The division has been removed.

The dissension has been overcome. The Bible says in verse 15 that the Lord hath "abolished in his flesh the enmity [hatred]" between the Jew and the Gentile (vs. 15).

There is a matter of DISTINCTION which has been overcome.

The Scripture says, "... of twain [that is, two]" He has made "one new man." That is why the Bible says that, "There is neither Greek nor Jew, circumcision nor uncircumcision, Barbarian, Scythian, bond nor free: but Christ is all, and in all" (Col. 3:11). All are one in Christ Jesus.

The Lord uses a symbol here He has made of two, a saved Jew and a saved Gentile, this one new man, which is a symbol or a picture of the church.

II. WHAT IS THIS NEW MAN LIKE?

Let us look at that new man, a representation of the church. First, he is a man of peace. I have already dealt with that. The Jew and the Gentile knew no peace. This is not talking about peace between man and God: God does that. "Therefore being justified by faith, we have peace with God through our Lord Jesus Christ" (Rom. 5:1). This is God talking about making peace between two kinds of people who have hated one another throughout all of history. Here we read this new man is a man of peace. He has peace not only with God but peace with every saved child of God. There is no distinction, no division, no distance barrier, no disunion, no dissension. There is peace because each has received peace from a common source, that is, Jesus Christ. "For he is our peace, who hath made both one, and hath broken down the middle wall of partition between us" (Eph. 2:14).

Second, this man is not only a man of peace, but he is a mysterious man. The Bible says the church is a mystery. This new man made of a Jew and a Gentile, these twain becoming one, is a mystery. When you read the word "mystery" in the Bible, don't let it bother you. A mystery in the Bible is not something we can't understand. A mystery in the Bible is something that for a period of time God did not make clear, did not give a full revelation of; but now He has.

Let me give you an illustration. When in I Corinthians 15:51 Paul said, "Behold, I shew you a mystery; We shall not all sleep, but we shall all be changed," he was talking about the second coming, when the Lord will come and a generation of Christians will still be alive. God did not make the full revelation of that altogether in the Old Testament. It was a mystery because it was hitherto unrevealed.

So is the church. There is no full revelation of a converted Jew and a converted Gentile becoming one in the body of Christ, no full revelation of it in the Old Testament. But it is in the New Testament and the Bible as a whole. So this man is a mysterious man. "Even the mystery which hath been hid from ages and from generations, but now is made manifest to his saints" (Col. 1:26).

Next, this new man is a reconciled man. The Scripture tells us in verse 16, "And that he might reconcile both." God is talking about Jew and Gentile. Let us see exactly what He is saying: "And that he might reconcile both unto God in one body by the cross, having slain the enmity [or hatred] thereby." This new man, made up of converted Jew and converted Gentile, which is the church, is a reconciled man. I have often thought it would be a good thing if we would have some Bible studies on "Great Words of Salvation." What does the word "salvation" mean? What does the word "justification" mean? What does the word "sanctification" mean? What does the word "reconciliation" mean?

The word "reconciliation" means "to change one person toward another." Wait a minute, God never changes. God is the same yesterday, today and forever. So this new man is one whose attitude toward God has been completely changed. God does not change. God changes men. The church is made up of people whom God has changed. I am sure there are a lot of folks who think they are in the church who are not. I would not make this reference to anyone here tonight. I believe that this church is made up mostly of saved people. But many think they are in the church who are not. Only changed people make up the church of Jesus Christ. Reconciliation means someone whom God has changed and made a new person in Christ Jesus. So, this man is a reconciled man. His attitude toward God has been changed.

In the fourth place—and I really like this. It is like the fellow who was kind of tongue-tied, with a hairlip or something. He couldn't talk plain. He couldn't say, "It gets sweeter and sweeter." He could only say, "It gets tweeter and tweeter." This gets "tweeter and tweeter" as we go!

The fourth thing about this man is, he has citizenship in Heaven. God is saying that this man is no more a stranger. I am talking about a new man, about a saved Jew, a saved Gentile made one in Christ. In verses 18 and 19 he said, "For through him we both have access by one Spirit unto the Father. Now therefore ye are no more strangers and foreigners [not like a Jew or a Gentile, but like a saint of God in the body], but fellowcitizens with the saints, and of the household of God."

A church member—and I am talking about a member of "the church," God's church, the body of Christ—is one whose citizenship is in Heaven. That is what Paul said in Philippians 3:20: "For our conversation [or citizenship] is in heaven: from whence also we look for the Saviour, the Lord Jesus Christ." This new man whose citizenship is in Heaven.

Actually our citizenship is in the United States. That is our "state." But I am talking about our "standing." Our position before God is that we are citizens of Heaven. Church people are citizens of another world.

Notice in closing. This man is a family man, for we read that this man is of the spiritual household of God. We sometimes speak of the church family. The church is like a family. There are those who, by age and experience, are like a father. There are those recently saved, who are immature, maybe like children. The church is like a family. In fact, Ephesians 3:15 says, "Of whom the whole family in heaven and earth is named."

The church is a family. We are family because we have the same Father. All of us bear the same name. "And the disciples were called *Christians* first in Antioch" (Acts 11:26). All of us have the same Father. Every one bears the same family name—Christian. That is the new man.

III. THE CHURCH IS A SPIRITUAL TEMPLE

Let us quickly look at the fourth and last symbol or representation of the church in the New Testament. That is, the church is a spiritual temple. Think about what we are saying. When we started to talk about the church, we spent a few minutes talking about what the church is not. We said the church is not a building. It is used as a place where people of God meet. "God dwelleth not in temples made with hands" (Acts 17:24). He dwells in human bodies.

Let me say this to you. Some of you are going to be a little shocked. The most overpious ones are going to say, "The preacher's gone crazy." That building across the road over there is as much a church as this building is. There is no such thing as a building being a church. Some of you even look shocked, because you are. Think about it. God dwelleth not in temples made with hands, and this church was made with hands, some of it with these two, grubby hands. God does not live in buildings.

When we say the church is a temple, we are saying, "God has said that the church is a spiritual temple." Let us look at it, starting with verse 20: "And are built upon the foundation of the apostles and prophets, Jesus Christ himself being the chief corner stone; In whom all the building fitly framed together groweth unto an holy temple in the Lord." So the church in the Bible is a holy temple, a spiritual temple.

This temple, thank God, has an Architect. If a person on the street undertakes to build a building of any significance without architectural plans, usually it would come out a mess. This spiritual temple has an Architect, that Architect spoken of in Matthew 16:18: "Upon this rock I will BUILD my church." In this Book God has laid out the blueprints for the building of a New Testament church. There can be no church built any other way. Jesus is the Architect. First Corinthians 3:9 says, "...ye are God's building." And I Corinthians 3:11 says, "For other foundation can no man lay than that is laid, which is Jesus Christ." The church is a spiritual building.

I think there is a reason why the Ephesian letter referred to the church. God gave Paul the words. Paul referred to the church as a spiritual building. Probably the most significant and beautiful building that ever existed on the face of the earth was in Ephesus. Some of us in this building have visited the ruins of Ephesus on the beautiful Mediterranean. In all of its prime and all of its pristine beauty there has never been a more beautiful city. It was built of stone but covered with white marble, so that the sun with its rays off the Mediterranean would cast its glint upon the beautiful city of solid white marble.

There is a theater there, the remains of an open theater, which seats 25,000. I have never seen anything like it. I experimented once when a group of us were there. I stood down in front of the lowest seats. Think now, 25,000 seats in a great open-air, no roof, no walls, an amphitheater. I spoke with less volume than I am speaking now. I had people on the top seat, way far away. I spoke to them like this. I asked them if they heard me. They answered me and conversed with me. They could tell me what I said. We heard each other without the slightest bit of strain. Ephesus was some city. There was probably never a more beautiful city in existence.

In that beautiful city was a certain temple called the Temple of Diana, built by the money and means and the genius of not just the Ephesians but of all Asia. It was a great headquarters, the mecca of those who worshiped the false goddess Diana. It was what Rome would be to a Catholic person tonight. The Temple of Diana was a magnificent thing. It was so beautiful that the Temple of Diana became a proverb throughout the whole known ancient world. I mean by that, if they wanted to say that something was beautiful or magnificent, they would use this temple as a proverb: "It is as beautiful as the Temple of Diana in Ephesus." It was a beautiful building.

When Paul wrote to this heathen city and visited it at least twice and spent three years there preaching, winning people to the Lord and bringing together a church of Jesus Christ, he pictured the church of the Lord as a spiritual temple.

First, I say, it has an Architect. Second, it is built durable and permanent. Jesus said, "Upon this rock I will build my church, and the gates of hell shall not prevail against it" (Matt. 16:18). Paul says here, "Jesus Christ himself being the chief corner stone" (Eph. 2:20).

Buildings in that day had not just a little stone like this one of ours. Ours has a date when this auditorium was built. Take away that stone, go down in the wall and you find a fruit jar or two with a lot of names of charter members, former members and so forth. That cornerstone of ours has nothing to do with the permanence of this building. It has nothing to do with its durability. It is more ornamental and more informative than anything else. But not so here at Ephesus. Cornerstones in a building in Paul's day were four huge cornerstones, all of which tied the walls together. Those cornerstones were the strength of the building and, you might say, the foundation of the whole temple. So, Paul said, "Jesus Christ himself being the chief corner stone."

When Peter was preaching in Acts 4, he was talking about Jesus. "This is the stone which was set at nought of you builders, which is become the head of the corner" (vs. 11). The chief cornerstone. It is built permanently. It is an edifice that rests upon the Son of God, and He is the most honorable stone in the whole structure. You and I are pictured as living stones being added to the great temple of Paul's time and of ours—the body of Christ.

This temple is built precisely and minutely. Look at the expression here about the church as a spiritual temple: "In whom all the building FITLY FRAMED TOGETHER..." (vs. 21).

I love to see a real carpenter at work. I can't build anything. I have broken as many as three things trying to fix one. I am not a builder, but I recognize a builder when I see one. A carpenter, a real craftsman, a cabinetmaker, can make a joint. You might say that he "mortises" it together. You can hardly tell that the joint is two pieces of material coming together. That is what I am talking about.

This spiritual temple is put together so precisely, so minutely, that the union of you and me together would not be noticeable to the human eye. We are one in Christ Jesus, "fitly framed together."

It is a growing temple. It is not yet finished. The last thing Paul mentions about it is, it is a growing temple: "...groweth unto an holy temple in the Lord" (Eph. 2:21). Acts 2:47 says, "And the Lord added to the church daily such as should be saved." If some were to get saved tonight, if some were to get saved next Sunday, the temple would grow a little more. The spiritual temple is getting larger all the time. It is unfinished. It is still growing. "...groweth unto an holy temple in the Lord."

The church is not only growing larger, but it is being made more pure. Some of these days it is going to be a completed temple without spot or wrinkle or blemish: "That he might present it to himself a glorious church, not having spot, or wrinkle, or any such thing; but that it should be holy and without blemish" (Eph. 5:27).

Then it is an occupied temple—verse 22: "In whom ye also are builded together for an habitation of God through the Spirit." God has always wanted a place to live on the earth. He said to Moses and the children of Israel in Exodus 25:8, "Let them make me a sanctuary; that I may dwell among them." He has that in the church. The church is where Jesus lives. I am talking about saved people. It is the habitation of God through the Spirit. Ye are the temple of the living God.

"And what agreement hath the temple of God with idols? for ye are the temple of the living God; as God hath said, I will dwell in them, and walk in them; and I will be their God, and they shall be my people."—II Cor. 6:16.

Chapter IV

The Lord's Supper

Matthew 26:17-30   I Corinthians 11:17-34

We will, God willing, spend several weeks on what we believe the Bible teaches on the subject of the church. We talked to you one evening on what we call the foundation of the church, showing from the Bible that the church is built on Jesus Christ, not on some man, not on a pope, not on a denomination. We have discussed four symbols used in the New Testament to represent the church and to help us see what the church is. We looked at the church as the BODY of Christ and the BRIDE of Christ. We looked at the church as a NEW MAN, then as a SPIRITUAL TEMPLE. We will continue, God willing, on Wednesday nights studying what the Bible teaches about the church.

One Wednesday night we will talk on church organization, how a church is to be organized. I think beyond any shadow of a doubt the Bible teaches how a church is to be organized. We will teach on the officers of the church, what the Bible teaches about a deacon. We will spend a Wednesday night talking about the Baptist deacon, the officers of the church.

We will spend a night talking about pastors. We have what you would call a plurality of pastors here in this church. That is perfectly scriptural. There is a precedent for that in the Bible. Why do some churches have one preacher and some have several pastors? We might even get on to the subject as to why some churches have no pastor!

Tonight we are going to discuss the ordinances of the church. We will try to show from the Scripture there are only two: the ordinance of the Lord's Supper and the ordinance of believer's baptism. Tonight we will talk about "The Ordinance of the Lord's Supper." Then, God willing, next Wednesday night we will speak on "The Ordinance of Believer's Baptism." Why do we baptize by immerson? Who is a candidate to baptize? What does baptism mean?

Tonight I will read from two sections of the New Testament, looking first at Matthew 26, then I Corinthians 11. Let us look together at Matthew 26 beginning with verse 17.

"Now the first day of the feast of unleavened bread the disciples came to Jesus, saying unto him, Where wilt thou that we prepare for thee to eat the passover? [The Lord's Supper is an outgrowth or a progression out of the passover supper.] *And he said, Go into the city to such a man, and say unto him, The Master saith, My time is at hand; I will keep the passover at thy house with my disciples."*

I will not speak on it tonight, but the passover meal lasted from one evening to the next evening, a period of 24 hours. The Lord Jesus ate the passover supper one night and became the Passover Lamb Himself the next day. This is the night before the crucifixion of Christ.

"And the disciples did as Jesus had appointed them; and they made ready the passover. Now when the even was come, he sat down with the twelve. And as they did eat, he said, Verily I say unto you, that one of you shall betray me. And they were exceeding sorrowful, and began every one of them to say unto him, Lord, is it I? And he answered and said, He that dippeth his hand with

me in the dish, the same shall betray me. The Son of man goeth as it is written of him: but woe unto that man by whom the Son of man is betrayed! it had been good for that man if he had not been born. Then Judas, which betrayed him, answered and said, Master, is it I? He said unto him, Thou hast said. And as they were eating, Jesus took bread, and blessed it, and brake it, and gave it to the disciples, and said, Take, eat; this is my body. And he took the cup, and gave thanks, and gave it to them, saying, Drink ye all of it: For this is my blood of the new testament, which is shed for many for the remission of sins. But I say unto you, I will not drink henceforth of this fruit of the vine, until that day when I drink it new with you in my Father's kingdom. And when they had sung an hymn, they went out into the mount of Olives."— Vss. 17-30.

Now let us read I Corinthians 11. We use this Scripture when we observe here the first Sunday of every month the Lord's Supper. It is just that, a supper. Some believe that it ought to be observed in the evening because the Bible speaks of it as a "supper."

Let us read some of these verses in I Corinthians 11. We will begin with verse 17 in this chapter.

"Now in this that I declare unto you I praise you not [Something is wrong about the way they were observing the Lord's Supper], *that ye come together not for the better, but for the worse. For first of all, when ye come together in the church, I hear that there be divisions among you; and I partly believe it. For there must be also heresies among you, that they which are approved may be made manifest among you. When ye come together therefore into one place, this is not to eat the Lord's supper. For in eating every one taketh before other his own supper: and one is hungry, and another is drunken. What? have ye not houses to eat and to drink in? or despise ye the church of God, and shame them that have not?* [This verse does not teach that it is wrong for Chris-

tians to eat in the Lord's house. He is talking about a perversion of the Lord's table.] *What shall I say to you? shall I praise you in this? I praise you not. For I have received of the Lord that which also I delivered unto you, That the Lord Jesus the same night in which he was betrayed took bread: And when he had given thanks, he brake it, and said, Take, eat: this is my body, which is broken for you: this do in remembrance of me. After the same manner also he took the cup, when he had supped, saying, This cup is the new testament in my blood: this do ye, as oft as ye drink it, in remembrance of me. For as often as ye eat this bread, and drink this cup, ye do shew the Lord's death till he come. Wherefore whosoever shall eat this bread, and drink this cup of the Lord, unworthily, shall be guilty of the body and blood of the Lord. But let a man examine himself, and so let him eat of that bread, and drink of that cup. For he that eateth and drinketh unworthily, eateth and drinketh damnation to himself, not discerning the Lord's body. For this cause many are weak and sickly among you, and many sleep. For if we would judge ourselves, we should not be judged. But when we are judged, we are chastened of the Lord, that we should not be condemned with the world. Wherefore, my brethren, when ye come together to eat, tarry one for another. And if any man hunger, let him eat at home; that ye come not together unto condemnation. And the rest will I set in order when I come."* — Vss. 17-34.

We believe there are two ordinances that the Lord Jesus Christ has given to be observed in His church: the ordinance of the Lord's Supper and the ordinance of believer's baptism. Some churches say there are three ordinances. They include what they call "the ordinance of foot-washing." But the Bible does not teach that foot-washing is an ordinance. When you see what the Bible says, you will know these are the only two ordinances. You will know also that foot-washing has never been established as an ordinance of the church.

I think foot-washing is a good practice, but not as an ordinance of the church. Go all the way back to chapter 18 of Genesis: there is the first mention in the Bible of the washing of feet. Three heavenly messengers came to Abraham as he sat under the oak tree in the plains of Mamre. Wanting to entertain them, Abraham said, "Sit here under the tree while I fetch water that your feet may be washed." This was an act of hospitality and friendliness. Come over to the Book of I Timothy 5:10. Paul is talking there about widows in the church, that is, people whose husbands have died and now the widows are the care of the church. He mentions some requirements for those widows: ". . . having been the wife of one man." "None are to be under 60 years of age." He mentioned their ministry to the people of God and he said, ". . . if she have washed the saints' feet. . . ." That is friendliness and brotherhood to the child of God.

Many believe that foot-washing is an ordinance because of reading John 13. That chapter is one of the four times in the New Testament where the ordinance of the Lord's Supper is described. Only in John does it mention foot-washing taking place when the Passover was observed and the Lord's Supper was established. Jesus went around the room, girded Himself with a towel, took a basin of water and washed the disciples' feet, then He said, "As I have done to you, so do ye one to another." There are folks who take that statement and say, "See? The Lord wants us to have a foot-washing like He had."

That is not true. When you study what Jesus was thinking about when He washed the disciples' feet prior to their partaking of the Passover Supper, you understand His actions. Peter says, "Lord, wash not only my feet, but also my hands and my head." Jesus said, "He that is washed needeth not save to wash his feet." He is saying, "If you are not cleansed, you can have no part with Me." Peter was already a Christian. All of the disciples except Judas were saved. Now the Lord is talking about the cleansing of Christians, cleansing from daily defilements and daily sin. He said, "You have already been bathed in the blood, so to speak; you are already a Christian—but your feet get dirty, like your soul gets dirty." So Jesus is saying to them, "I am cleansing you from daily defilement."

If I were to wash your feet and you were to wash mine, neither of us could say, "I am cleansing you from the sin you have gotten on your soul." You and I cannot do that. Foot-washing today would not mean what it meant when Jesus instituted it.

Now think of this. First, cleansing from sin for a believer has a spiritual meaning: "Jesus saith to him, He that is washed [bathed] needeth not save to wash [rinse] his feet, but is clean every whit: and ye are clean, but not all." The first use of the word "wash" in this verse means to bathe; the second use of the word means to rinse. It was never, never practiced by the apostles in the Book of Acts. Not one mention is made that the apostles ever practiced foot-washing as an ordinance. More than that, it is not taught in the Pauline Epistles. All of us know that what we call "the Pauline Epistles" are also called "Church Epistles." Nowhere in Church Epistles is foot-washing taught as an ordinance. It is not mentioned one time in the biblical history of the early church. So Jesus was not establishing an ordinance when He washed the disciples' feet, when He instituted the first Lord's Supper. So we say that there are only two ordinances: the Lord's Supper and believer's baptism.

I. THE LORD'S SUPPER, AN OUTGROWTH OF THE PASSOVER SUPPER

Let us look at the Lord's Supper, which is an outgrowth of the

Passover Supper. In that wonderful chapter, Exodus 12, we see the Lord is about to deliver His people out of the bondage of Egypt. He is going to do it by blood, so to speak. He has sent plague after plague. No plague, no judgment ever delivered one single Israelite from the bondage of Egypt; but blood did. Finally God said, 'Now you take and slay a lamb. ''. . . and without shedding of blood is no remission'' (Heb. 9:22). Sprinkle the blood on the lintel of the door and the two posts. When I pass over tonight in judgment, I will slay the firstborn of every home where there is NO BLOOD. When I pass over the home where the blood is sprinkled, I will spare the firstborn of that home.' That is where we get the word ''passover.''

God said this lamb had to be without spot or blemish because it typified the perfect Lamb of God, the Lord Jesus Christ. Its blood was shed, its body was consumed. Not a bone of it was to be broken, just like no bones of Jesus were broken on the cross when ordinarily they would have been. The Roman soldier came to break the legs of crucifixion victims to be sure that they were dead. But when he came to Jesus, he said, ''He is dead already.'' He could not break the Word of God, for the Word of God had said, ''A bone of him shall not be broken'' (John 19:36).

But of the passover lamb, God said, ''Someday when your children are going to ask, 'What means this visible thing, this tangible thing that you are doing? What means this Passover Supper?' you remind them that they were delivered from Egypt by the blood of the passover lamb.''

''. . . and when I see the blood, I will pass over you.''

That lamb looked in two different directions—backward to deliverance from Egypt and forward to the coming of the true Lamb of God. You see, that lamb was a type. It looked backward to deliverance from Egypt. It looked backward to deliverance and redemption and looked forward to the coming of the Lord Jesus

Christ to die for our sins. "Behold the Lamb of God, which taketh away the sin of the world" (John 1:29).

The same thing is true of the Lord's Supper. The Lord's Supper looks two ways. When Paul wrote to the Corinthian church he said, "For as often as ye this bread, and drink this cup, YE DO SHEW THE LORD'S DEATH..." (I Cor. 11:26). That is looking backward to a finished work, a blood work on the cross. "....ye do shew the Lord's death TILL HE COME." That is pointing to His second coming, as the passover lamb pointed to His first coming. I am simply saying that the Lord's Supper is an outgrowth of the Passover Supper. We will not understand it unless we see it as such.

There are some who even believe that it has never changed, that it is still the same as the Passover. That, of course, could not possibly be true. God has never told us to slay a lamb. God has never told us to put a lamb aside for three days and scrutinize it, as the Lord was scrutinized for three years. God never told us to do that, nor to slay the lamb and sprinkle the blood. That has already been done on the cross. "For it is not possible that the blood of bulls and of goats should take away sins" (Heb. 10:4). The Lord's Supper is an outgrowth of the Passover Supper.

II. THE MEANING OF THE LORD'S SUPPER

What does the Lord's Supper mean? A man called the other night, telling me the sad story you hear so many times. It was a problem in his church, a deacon who believed that the Lord's Supper should be observed with fermented wine, not just the fruit of the vine. He said, "Every time we have communion, this deacon leaves. He will not partake of it. We know that God does not want us to use fermented wine."

Let me say that the Bible never contradicts itself, never. God said, "Look not thou upon the wine when it is red, when it giveth his colour in the cup, when it moveth itself aright" (Prov. 23:31). God never contradicts Himself. There is a generic term for wine in the New Testament. It is like when Jesus turned the water into wine at the marriage feast, it was not fermented liquid. A generic term *oinos* is used which sometimes means, "a liquid made from grapes." This generic term does not always mean a fermented substance. It is like grape juice. There is misunderstanding by thousands about what communion, the Lord's Supper, really means.

Take, for instance, a Catholic doctrine. I am not up here to attack the Catholic church. But the Catholic church believes in "transubstantiation." The Catholics say there are seven ordinances. The Catholic church says that the bread actually becomes the body of Jesus and the wine literally becomes the blood of Jesus Christ.

One can see where folks might think that. When Jesus handed them the bread and instituted the Supper, He said, "Take, eat; this is my body." When He handed them the cup, He said, "Drink ye all of it; For this is my blood."

Now wait a minute. In John 6, at that great miracle of feeding the five thousand, He said to the people, "Except ye eat the flesh of the Son of man, and drink his blood, ye have no life in you" (vs. 53). But Jesus did not say, "You have to eat this flesh and drink this blood." You see, the Bible also says that man is not to drink blood in the Old Testament.

When Jesus was teaching the parable about sowing the Word of God, He said, "The field is the world." That field was not really the world; it just represented the world. When He said, "The seed you sow is the Word of God," that seed did not become the Bible, the Word of God; it just represented the Bible. And that is what God is talking about when He says, 'This broken element represents My body.' This fruit of the vine represents the blood shed upon the cross of Calvary. No Christian who believes the

Bible, and sees the Lord and hears one illustration after another to teach the truth, could ever say that when we take communion, it actually becomes the body of Jesus and that we are drinking the blood of Jesus Christ.

What is the Lord's Supper? It is a memorial, Jesus said. Paul taught that also. Notice when he wrote to the Corinthian believers he gave the order and meaning of the Lord's table. "When he [Jesus] had given thanks, he brake it [bread], and said,...this do in remembrance of me....he took the cup...saying,...this do in remembrance of me." It is a memorial, a living, visible, tangible memorial of what the Lord Jesus Christ has done for us on the cross. Twice He said, "This do in remembrance of me."

III. THE PURPOSE OF THE LORD'S SUPPER

The Lord's Supper has a purpose. I hope we will remember it when we partake of the Lord's Supper.

By the way, the Lord's Supper is the LORD'S Supper. I say that for this reason. Some Baptist churches would say, "Now, Mr. Malone, we are observing the Lord's Supper, but we cannot let you partake with us because the Lord's Supper is for the members of this church." No; the Lord's Supper is the LORD'S SUPPER. And the Lord's Supper is for the Lord's people. It is not for the unsaved. Remember Judas? When Jesus said, "One of you will betray me. One of you is a devil.... He it is who dippeth his hand with me in the dish," they were observing the Passover Supper. Judas asked, "Is it I?" Jesus said, "Thou sayest it." John 13:30 says that Judas went out and it was night. Judas never partook of the Lord's Supper. He had no right because he was lost. It is for any saved person, any child of God.

I had a meeting one time with a dear preacher friend of mine who believed that only a member of that church had any right to partake of the Lord's Supper. And he made that known in the meeting.

When the meeting was over, I said to this dear man of God, "Now if I ever come to your church and you are serving the Lord's Supper, I'm going to partake." I didn't know what he would say. He kind of leaned over to me and said, "Dr. Malone, if you come to my church and we are serving communion, I sure want you to partake of it with us." I thought, *He does not have a very strong conviction!* Rightly so. It has no foundation, no basis.

The purpose of the Lord's Supper is threefold.

We look BACKWARD to a finished work. When we sit together at this table the Christian can look back to the cross to hear Him cry, "It is finished!" (John 19:30). Our sins have been paid for completely. We look back to a finished and completed work.

We look INWARDLY. Notice Paul said, "But let a man examine himself. . ." (I Cor. 11:28). When we partake of the Lord's Supper, it should be a time when a Christian asks himself, *Is there unconfessed sin in my life?* Folks, many a Christian has what I call "sins of the spirit." They have not robbed a bank or killed anybody, or stolen any money, but they have sins of the spirit. They are envious, jealous. They have hatred, ill-will. They have malice in their heart. This is just as much a sin as any sin! When a Christian comes to the table of the Lord, Paul said, "Look inward." Not only look backward to the finished work, but look inward. "Let a man examine himself." "Search me, O God, and know my heart: try me, and know my thoughts: And see if there be any wicked way in me, and lead me in the way everlasting" (Ps. 139:23, 24).

I saw that happen in this church once. I could not keep the tears back. I saw a man come to this communion table years ago who had something in his heart, an ill, wrong feeling toward another man sitting at that table. While the people were coming down the aisles and we were in preparation to start administering the Supper of the Lord, I stood right by him. I heard him reach over and

say, "Brother So-and-So, I want you to forgive me for the things
I said to you. I was wrong. Will you please forgive me?" The
good brother said, "Yes, I will." And they partook of the Lord's
Supper. "Let a man examine himself." Not only looking backward
to a finished work, but look inward for heart-searching. God knows
tonight that we need heart-searching! We need examination to see
if we are in fellowship with Jesus Christ.

There is another look, the UPWARD look. "For as often as
ye eat this bread, and drink this cup, ye do shew the Lord's death
till he come" (I Cor. 11:26). When we sit at the table of the Lord,
we say, "We are looking for the coming of the Lord Jesus Christ!"
"Even so, come Lord Jesus" (Rev. 22:20).

IV. THE PENALTIES OF PARTAKING
IN AN UNWORTHY MANNER

Notice another thing or two, and I am through. There are some
penalties described in I Corinthians 11 for partaking of the Lord's
Supper unworthily. When Paul says, "For he that eateth and
drinketh unworthily, eateth and drinketh damnation [condemna-
tion] to himself," he is not saying that if that Christian has some
sin or is not perfect, that he is partaking unworthily. That is not
what this verse teaches. To partake of it unworthily is to abuse
it, as these people did. Some made it a feast of drunkenness. Some
came and ate until they were full, while some of the poor sat back,
hungry. A Christian is to search his heart. But that is not what
this is talking about. Rather, it is talking of the Supper of the Lord
as He describes it: "What shall I say to you? shall I praise you
in this? I praise you not."

There are some results of partaking of the Supper unworthily.
There is debility, disease and death. "For this cause [perverting
the Lord's table] many are weak [debility] and sickly [diseased]."

Now it does not mean every time one gets sick, God is punishing him. Why do most people get sick? Because that is a part of life. Our frail, human bodies do not last long. When you see a saint of God sick, don't think: *I wonder what he's done wrong now, that the Lord is having to spank him.*

But God does send sickness, Paul says, for perversions of the table of the Lord: "For this cause, many are weak and sickly, and many sleep." God even takes some prematurely to Heaven because they have perverted the table of the Lord. So it is important.

It is serious, yet beautiful, to sit together and look backward to the cross, and forward to the coming of our blessed Lord.

I have already alluded to the fact that it is for saved people. Judas went out before Jesus instituted the Lord's Supper. So just the child of God can partake of either ordinance. Only a Christian can partake of communion. Only a Christian can be baptized. You do not partake of communion in order to be saved; you partake of it because you are saved. You do not get baptized in order to be saved; you get baptized because you have been saved.

The table of the Lord is to be observed regularly by the church. God does not say how often but He does say, "For as often as ye eat this bread, and drink this cup, ye do shew the Lord's death till he come."

V. THE PEOPLE OF THE LORD'S SUPPER

We have already alluded to the fact that Judas left the table. "He then having received the sop went immediately out: and it was NIGHT" (John 13:30). It has been NIGHT ever since in the dark soul of Judas. He knew nothing of the love that Jesus spoke of in verse 35: "By this shall all men know that ye are my disciples, if ye have love one to another." He sang no hymn, as the others did, at the close of the Supper. He knew nothing of the meaning of the broken body and shed blood of the Lord Jesus Christ. Those at the Lord's table are a blood-washed, born-again people. They feel His outflow of love and they love one another. They experience a glorious unity unspoiled by sin and carnality.

What a sweet hour when we come together for the love of the saints and the glory of the Saviour!

Chapter V

Believer's Baptism

Luke 3:1-22

Tonight we will talk about the ordinance of baptism. It will take two Wednesday nights to cover this subject. I will spend some time on what we might call erroneous baptism, that is, people thinking they are being baptized when they are sprinkled. Then being baptized for the dead, as the Bible mentions it. Then being baptized before you are saved, then not being baptized after you are saved—erroneous baptism.

I will spend some time on the baptism of the Lord Jesus Christ. It is very important. It says a lot to us. The baptism of Jesus has a very special meaning. He did not get baptized because He had been converted. He has always been Jesus and divine, has always been God.

Tonight we are going to look at believer's baptism, the second of the two ordinances that we are discussing. I am sure that if you were to ask a lot of Baptists how one is to be baptized, what mode is proper, they would answer, "Be baptized by immersion in water after you are saved."

But suppose some did not think that the proper way to be baptized and they said to you, "Show me in the Bible where sprinkling is wrong, where infant baptism is wrong. Show me in the Bible where it teaches that you are to be baptized by immersion."

I am afraid some Baptist Christians could not do that.

Once I preached both morning and night on baptism. We mention it a lot. We practice it all of the time. But maybe we do not teach it as much as we ought.

I read tonight from the Book of Luke, chapter 3. May the Lord speak to our hearts out of the blessed Word of God. This has to do primarily with the ministry of John the Baptist and a little bit about the baptism of Jesus.

"Now in the fifteenth year of the reign of Tiberius Caesar, Pontius Pilate being governor of Judaea, and Herod being tetrarch of Galilee, and his brother Philip tetrarch of Ituraea and of the region of Trachonitis, and Lysanias the tetrarch of Abilene. Annas and Caiaphas being the high priests, the word of God came unto John the son of Zacharias in the wilderness. [This is important. John baptized before Calvary. Did he do it under God's direction? He certainly did.] *And he came into all the country about Jordan, preaching the baptism of repentance for the remission of sins; As it is written in the book of the words of Esaias the prophet, saying, The voice of one crying in the wilderness, Prepare ye the way of the Lord, make his paths straight. Every valley shall be filled, and every mountain and hill shall be brought low; and the crooked shall be made straight, and the rough ways shall be made smooth; and all flesh shall see the salvation of God. Then said he to the multitude that came forth to be baptized of him, O generation of vipers, who hath warned you to flee from the wrath to come? Bring forth therefore fruits worthy of repentance, and begin not to say within yourselves, We have Abraham to our father: for I say unto you, That God is able of these stones to raise up children unto Abraham. And now also the axe is laid unto the root of the trees: every tree therefore which bringeth not forth good fruit is hewn down, and cast into the fire.* [He is talking to people who came to be baptized but had not repented. 'Bring forth fruits

of repentance, then you can be baptized.' Then he uses an illustration. 'A tree that does not bring forth fruit is hewn down, cast into the fire.'] *And the people asked him, saying, What shall we do then? He answereth and saith unto them, He that hath two coats, let him impart to him that hath none; and he that hath meat, let him do likewise. Then came also publicans to be baptized, and said unto him, Master, what shall we do? And he said unto them, Exact no more than that which is appointed you.* [He wants to see the fruits of repentance before people are to be baptized.] *And the soldiers likewise demanded of him, saying, And what shall we do? And he said unto them, Do violence to no man, neither accuse any falsely; and be content with your wages. And as the people were in expectation, and all men mused in their hearts of John, whether he were the Christ, or not; John answered, saying unto them all, I indeed baptize you with water; but one mightier than I cometh, the latchet of whose shoes I am not worthy to unloose: he shall baptize you with the Holy Ghost and with fire: Whose fan is in his hand, and he will throughly purge his floor, and will gather the wheat into his garner; but the chaff he will burn with fire unquenchable. And many other things in his exhortation preached he unto the people. But Herod the tetrarch, being reproved by him for Herodias his brother Philip's wife, and for all the evils which Herod had done, Added yet this above all, that he shut up John in prison. Now when all the people were baptized, it came to pass, that Jesus also being baptized, and praying, the heaven was opened, And the Holy Ghost descended in a bodily shape like a dove upon him, and a voice came from heaven, which said, Thou art my beloved Son; in thee I am well pleased."*— Vss. 1-22.

Let us repeat three verses as kind of a starting point. Verse 16: "John answered, saying unto them all, I indeed baptize you with water. . . ."

Notice verses 21 and 22, the baptism of Jesus: "Now when all the people were baptized, it came to pass, that Jesus also being baptized, and praying, the heaven was opened, And the Holy Ghost descended in a bodily shape like a dove upon him, and a voice came from heaven, which said, Thou art my beloved Son; in thee I am well pleased."

I would like to spend time on the baptism of Jesus, which we will not do tonight. But I will say that it certainly is given tremendous significance in the Bible. The virgin birth of Jesus, His conception by the Holy Ghost in the womb of the virgin Mary is not discussed in all four of the Gospels, yet nothing in the world could be more important. There are some miracles that Jesus did which all of the Gospels do not give record. In fact, there is only one miracle that Jesus wrought that all four of the gospel writers do record—the miracle of the feeding of the five thousand men. But it is interesting to note that all four of the gospel writers give emphasis and significance to the baptism in water of our Lord Jesus Christ.

Three truths come to us immediately for an introduction to the study on believer's baptism in water. First, the Bible tells us that it was instituted by John. John was called of God. He was the Lord's man, God's preacher. John preached that people had to repent and believe in order to be saved. Then John the Baptist baptized them in water after they had repented and were saved. So baptism in the New Testament was instituted by John.

Then, it was observed by Jesus Christ. Some of us have been to that beautiful spot near the ruins of the city of Jericho, where the River Jordan soon enters into the Dead Sea. Just before it enters into the Dead Sea is the traditional spot where it is said that Jesus was baptized. He came to John and said, "Baptize Me." John said to Jesus, "I have need to be baptized of thee." What John was saying was this: "I baptize you with water, but there cometh one after me who shall baptize you with the Holy Ghost." John says, "Jesus, You ought to baptize me rather than me baptize You." But our Lord said, "Suffer it to be so, for thus it becometh us to fulfill all righteousness." John baptized Jesus Christ.

We can say, first of all, it was instituted by John. Second, it was observed by Jesus Christ.

It was not only instituted by John the Baptist and observed by Jesus Christ, but without any doubt, it has been practiced by the Bible-believing church for 2,000 years without change. On the day of Pentecost men were convicted in their hearts of their sin and they cried out, "Men and brethren, what shall we do?" Acts 2:38 answers, "Repent, and be baptized every one of you in the name of Jesus Christ for the remission of sins. . . ." Then Acts 2:41 says, "Then they that gladly received the word were baptized; and the same day there were added unto them about three thousand souls." So, the church has, from the day of Pentecost until now, practiced believer's baptism by immersion in water.

There is a lot of discussion on baptism. I was introduced to it even before I was saved. When I was eleven years old, I wanted with all my heart to be saved. (I got saved at the age of nineteen.) I wanted Christ in my life and the forgiveness of sins. I went forward in the First Methodist Church of Russellville, Alabama. The evangelist was a red-headed preacher. I went and gave my hand to the pastor and the evangelist and said, "I want to be saved." They put their hand on my head, shook my hand and said, "Come back next Sunday and be baptized."

I went back the next Sunday and they took a chalice of water, sprinkled a little on my head and received me into the membership of the church.

I went out as lost as I went in. What they were virtually saying is, "This sprinkling, this so-called baptism, is all you need in order to be a Christian." I was not saved and for eight more years I lived in darkness and sin, with a hungering heart to know the Lord. There is so much error about baptism.

In the Bible, "baptism" is a "coined" word. Actually it is not the true translation of the word for baptize that is in the Bible. I do not have anything but the King James Bible, and do not want anything but the King James. I love it. Please do not come up and say, "You said something questionable about the King James Version." There were eighty-eight scholars of King James and they were Anglican. They did not believe in baptism by immersion. So when they came to the word *baptizo*, the Greek word for baptism which means to dip under or to immerse, they put this word "baptism" in the English translation, which does not indicate what the mode of baptism is. The King James translators translated the word exactly as it was in the Textus Receptus. They translated or Anglicized the word *baptizo* into baptism, which is correct. The word in the New Testament *baptizo* not only speaks of baptism but tells the only way that baptism can be administered, that is, to dip under or to immerse in water. When the Greeks referred to dipping a garment into a solution to dye it, or dipping a small vessel into a larger vessel of water, they used the word *baptizo*.

Some say, "The Bible mentions sprinkling." But never in reference to baptism. For instance, Hebrews 9:13 mentions the sprinkling of blood. That is another Greek word, *rhantizo*, which is never used in reference to water baptism. The Bible says only one thing: that baptism means immersion in water. There are not two forms or three, but only one way to be baptized, and that is by immersion in water.

The ordinance of the Lord's Supper speaks of His death. Now here is the second ordinance. What does it mean? To what does it refer when one is baptized in this baptistry having been saved? What is that ritual, that act, that ordinance? What is it saying when a Christian is baptized?

It is a demonstration of the Gospel. As the Lord's Supper demonstrates His death, His broken body, His shed blood, the believer's baptism demonstrates the Gospel. Let me read you the definition of the Gospel and you will see what I am saying is absolutely true. Look at I Corinthians 15:1-4:

"Moreover, brethren, I declare unto you the gospel which I preached unto you, which also ye have received, and wherein ye stand; By which also ye are saved, if ye keep in memory what I preached unto you, unless ye have believed in vain. For I delivered unto you first of all that which I also received, how that Christ died for our sins according to the scriptures: And that he was buried, and that he rose again the third day according to the scriptures."

So the Bible definition of the Gospel is the DEATH and the BURIAL and the RESURRECTION of Jesus Christ.

When a believer is baptized, he is giving a picture of the Gospel. When he is put down into the water, it is his identification with the death of Jesus Christ. He is buried in the waves of baptism. He is raised to walk in newness of life. Every time a convert is baptized, he is giving a living pictorial of the Gospel of the Lord Jesus Christ.

As the Lord's Supper speaks of His death, the ordinance of baptism speaks of the Gospel by which we are saved. Romans 6 bears that out:

"Therefore we are buried with him by baptism into death: that like as Christ was raised up from the dead by the glory of the Father, even so we also should walk in newness of life. For if we have been planted together in the likeness of his death, we shall be also in the likeness of his resurrection."—Vss. 4, 5.

Verse 4 says we have been BURIED—that is, immersed.

Verse 5 says if we have been PLANTED with Him, we shall also be raised with Him.

Baptism is a picture of the Gospel.

I. WHO IS TO BE BAPTIZED?

Let us answer from the Bible some things that we put in question form.

First, who is to be baptized? There is a reason why we ought to clarify who should be baptized. When Peter went to the house of Cornelius and preached the Gospel to that great household, people were saved. Peter said, "Can any man forbid water that these should not be baptized?" (Acts 10:47). Who would keep these converts from being baptized? There was a question raised as to whether they should be baptized.

The Bible gives the answer. Only believers should be baptized. In Matthew 3:7, 8 we read some wonderful truths that will help us to see that only a believer is to be baptized. It is a repetition of what we read in chapter 3 of Luke when they came to John and said to him, "Baptize us." He said, "Bring forth fruit meet for repentance before I will baptize you." Only saved people are to be baptized. Notice Acts 2:41 again, "Then they that gladly received his word were baptized...." No one is to be baptized until he repents and receives the Word of God. When these gladly received the Word of God, then they were baptized.

Acts 8:12 is the account of the great revival that Philip held in Samaria. In that great revival, we learn a great deal about baptism. Acts 8:12 says, "But when they believed Philip preaching the things concerning the kingdom of God, and the name of Jesus Christ, they were baptized, both men and women." Never is there any teaching in the Bible that anyone had a right to be baptized until he repents and believes in the Lord Jesus Christ.

Also in that same chapter the Spirit of God told Philip to go and join himself to the chariot of the Ethiopian eunuch who was reading what we know now is Isaiah 53. The Bible says that Philip began at the same Scripture and preached unto him Jesus. The man asked, "Of whom is the prophet speaking here? Of himself or of some other man?" Philip "began at the same scripture and preached unto him Jesus."

As they rode along, they came to an oasis in the desert. The Ethiopian eunuch said, "See, here is water; what doth hinder me from being baptized?" Philip said, "If thou believest with all thine heart that Jesus is the Son of God, thou mayest." The Ethiopian eunuch said, "I believe that Jesus is the Son of God." Then they went down into the water and the eunuch was baptized.

No one has the right to baptism but believers. The whole picture here is one of a believer being baptized by immersion.

Notice that all believers are to be baptized. I do not believe that baptism saves a person. I do not believe that not being baptized will keep a person out of Heaven. The thief on the cross was saved and never got baptized, but he never had a chance to be. I believe any person who owns the name of Jesus ought to follow the Lord in baptism. Only believers should be baptized. And all believers should be baptized. Why? Jesus gave the Great Commission in Matthew 28:18-20:

"And Jesus came and spake unto them, saying, All power is given unto me in heaven and in earth. Go ye therefore, and teach all nations, baptizing them in the name of the Father, and of the Son, and of the Holy Ghost: Teaching them to observe all things whatsoever I have commanded you...."

He just gave a commandment, "Go and disciple people and baptize them!" Baptism is a command of Jesus. He did not leave it up to us, now that we are saved and going to Heaven, to decide whether or not we will be baptized. He puts it so squarely as a commandment that a person has to disobey God if he refuses to be baptized by immersion in water.

There is no instance in the Book of Acts where believers were not baptized. There is not one instance in the whole Book of Acts where a believer ever got saved who did not follow the Lord in baptism. That says to me that all believers are to be baptized. I believe this very strongly.

Some believers got baptized under some very extreme circumstances. There were Paul and Silas in the Philippian jail. The Bible says that at midnight they sang praises unto God. Then after that an earthquake came. The prison was destroyed and the jailer was convicted. All after midnight. The jailer fell down at their feet and said, "Sirs, what must I do to be saved?" They answered, "Believe on the Lord Jesus Christ, and thou shalt be saved, and thy house." "And he [the jailer] took them the same hour of the night, and washed their stripes; and was baptized, he and all his, straightway" (Acts 16:30, 31, 33). This was after midnight. You can't have an earthquake, get things cleaned up and get out very quickly, so it took a little while. It might have been two or three in the morning.

Here is a man whose family got saved. Paul and Silas did not say, "Wait a while and think about it and pray about it, then get baptized." No. Under extreme circumstances a man and his family believed in the Lord and were baptized right on the spot.

I do not believe in *infant* baptism, but I sure do believe in *instant* baptism.

II. WHY SHOULD A BELIEVER BE BAPTIZED?

Why is a believer to be baptized? I have already alluded to the Great Commission. Jesus commanded us to disciple people and get them baptized. Here is another great reason. Our Lord was baptized, but not for the same reason you and I were. We were baptized because we were lost sinners. We believed and were saved and we wanted to do what would please God and what the Bible teaches, so we got baptized. But Jesus is our example. When John was reluctant, Jesus said, "Suffer it to be so now, for thus it becometh us to fulfill all righteousness." If I had no other reason than that, it would be reason enough.

Do you want to be like Jesus? Do you want to follow Jesus? Do you want to be worthy of the name of a "Christian," one belonging to Christ? Then do what He did. Jesus was baptized as an example to us.

Baptism shows our identification with the church body. You ask some folks the definition of a church and they will answer, "A church is a group of baptized believers." I guess that is right. I have heard a lot of people argue about it. I think I even saw two preachers fight about it one time! I do not mean "fuss," I mean "fight." You know like fist-to-face? So there is a lot of argument about it. The Bible does teach that baptism identifies us with a certain body of people.

Look at Acts 2:41 again: "Then they that gladly received his word were baptized; and the same day there were added unto them about three thousand souls." These people who were baptized were believers, of course. Then they were baptized and were added unto the church body. One great man I know says, "Baptism is identification with the Lord in His death, burial and resurrection and identification with the church of the Lord Jesus Christ."

Every believer ought to be baptized in obedience to the Bible. A Christian should be baptized in order to show outwardly what has taken place inwardly.

III. WHEN SHOULD A BELIEVER BE BAPTIZED?

I have already said that we believe in *instant* baptism. There is no probationary period set forth in the Bible. A man of God who spent eighteen years on the mission field stood right in this church one time and said to me, "Preacher, on the mission field we wouldn't dare do what you are doing in this church, that is, when people get saved, baptize them. We have to have a probationary period. We wait six weeks, then we baptize them."

I said to my dear brother, "Is there some Bible teaching about that?"

He said, "No, but it's logical. It's practical."

You do not get that out of the Bible. I would much rather be scriptural than be humanly logical. There is no such thing as a probationary period set forth in the Bible. Acts 2:41, just referred to, says, "...the same day there were added unto them...." On the day of Pentecost they got baptized. I referred to Acts 16:33; it says, "...the same hour of the night...." they got baptized.

Somebody says, "Paul waited three days before he got baptized." So what? Paul had an unusual conversion. He was smitten with blindness. In a way his was no more miraculous than mine or yours. I know of a fellow who was sitting under a railroad trestle. Someone had given him a tract and he read it sitting under a railroad trestle and got saved. So he would try to get others to come and sit under the railroad trestle so they could get saved.

Some people weep when they get saved. Some do not shed a tear. Some people shout when they get saved. Some do not utter a word. Some kneel to get saved. Some stand and trust the Lord. Paul waited three days because for three days he could not see until God sent a special messenger to him, Ananias. Ananias said, "Brother Paul, arise and be baptized and be filled with the Holy Ghost." The Bible says that the scales fell from his eyes and he was baptized.

I will tell you what you do. If anytime anybody gets saved and goes blind and is blind for three days, then you can wait three days before baptizing him. But if he does not go blind, that is no excuse to wait. Paul went blind and three days alone, still in repentance, waited upon God. That is not a Bible example; it is a slight delay of Paul's getting baptized.

I have lots of questions, but our time is up. So we will close right here tonight on our teaching of baptism and take it up later. Someone here tonight might not be satisfied with your baptism. I know some who are not. It is just like my experience. I was sprinkled when I was eleven. Of course, that is not baptism. In 1935 I got saved, at age nineteen. I went up to Bob Jones University, an undenominational school. They did not teach it one way or the other. There were Methodists, Baptists, Presbyterians and other denominations represented there. I had read the New Testament just before I got saved. I had read it through in about three days. When I got saved in August, 1935, I turned right around and read the New Testament again in two or three days. In September I began to really wonder what I should do about it. You see, I was saved in the Methodist church. I had no instruction—just reading the Bible and seeing what it said.

One day I looked up an ordained Baptist preacher and I said to him, "I want to be baptized by immersion. You are an ordained Baptist preacher. I want you to baptize me." So Brother Harden and I one morning at about 5 o'clock walked a mile and a quarter from the campus out to a lake. By then it was October. Leaves were on the water. We waded out into the water and raked the leaves aside. Then we stood and held each other's hand and prayed. We asked God to bless us. He baptized me in that lake. I have never doubted from that moment until this that I have obeyed God in the matter of believer's baptism.

IV. WHAT IS THE MODE OF BAPTISM?

We asked the question, "Who is to be baptized?" We let the

Bible answer. Second, we asked the question, "Why should a believer be baptized?" We let the Bible answer. Third, we asked the question, "When should a believer be baptized?" We let the Bible answer. Three other questions, God willing, we will deal with, also.

What is the mode of baptism? I want to spend some time on that, showing that the English word for baptism in the King James Bible is from the Greek word *baptizo* which means "to immerse, to submerge, to dip under." That is the meaning of "baptism" in the New Testament. There is no reference in the Old Testament as such. Believer's baptism is a New Testament teaching. But *tabal*, a Hebrew word, is synonymous with the Greek word *baptizo*. That word also in the Old Testament means "to immerse, to submerge, to dip under." The meaning of that word is illustrated in the Old Testament in the story of Joseph and his brethren.

Joseph is a type of Christ. Joseph's brethren put him in a pit and later decided not to leave him there, but to pretend that he was dead. This is recorded in Genesis 37:31. They took a goat, killed it and caught the blood. The Scriptures use this word *tabal* which means to submerge, and they dipped it in blood. The word means "to submerge, immerse, dip under" whenever it is found in the Bible. A similar Hebrew word is also used in the Old Testament for the "dipping" of Naaman.

I have already mentioned that Jesus was immersed. We tried to show that the Ethiopian eunuch was baptized by immersion, the only mode that pictures the Gospel. Let us take it right there and go a little further on the mode of baptism, though we have already spent considerable time on it. The terms used in the New Testament in reference to baptism teach immersion. Let us look at Romans 6:3-5:

"Know ye not, that so many of us as were baptized into Jesus Christ were baptized into his death? Therefore we are buried with

him by baptism into death: [listen to the language] *that like as Christ was raised up from the dead by the glory of the Father, even so we also should walk in newness of life."*

Here the Bible is saying that believers are baptized into His death and buried with Him in baptism. When we bury or use the word "buried," we are inferring a number of things that have to be true. First, "buried" implies that one is dead. Let us not be like some folks who, when they say they are going to "Mr. Jones' funeral," invariably are asked, "Did he die?" You feel like saying, "No, we're going to bury him alive." Burying implies that one has died.

So does baptism. That is what the Scripture is saying. Being buried in baptism is for one who is united with Christ in His death. The Bible says that we are crucified with Christ. We are buried with Him in baptism. It is a picture of the death, burial and resurrection of Jesus. Baptism is a burial that says we also have died in Christ Jesus.

Burial always implies that one is covered up. Burial means, when used in reference to baptism, that one, some way or another, is covered up. People who believe in sprinkling ought never, if they are going to be consistent, bury somebody under the ground and cover him up. They ought to just say, "This person is dead," sprinkle a little dirt on him and leave him where he is. Oh, no! That does not fit, because sprinkling does not fit. Burial in the Bible implies that one is covered up.

Burial always precedes resurrection. That means that no sinner who does not have life has a right to be baptized.

Burial also implies a severance, a separation from the world. Dead people have been cut off from this world and its way of living. Baptism is saying, "You are dead with Christ. You have been buried with Christ. You are separated unto Christ. You are looking for the day when He shall raise us from the dead."

Paul uses the word "buried." There are terms in the Bible used in reference to baptism that teach, beyond any doubt, that the mode of baptism is by immersion, submersion, or dipping in water.

Let us see it in another place or two. John said, "I indeed baptize you with water; but one mightier than I cometh, the latchet of whose shoes I am not worthy to unloose: he shall baptize you with the Holy Ghost and with fire" (Luke 3:16). That was fulfilled on the day of Pentecost. We read these words in Acts 2:2, "And suddenly there came a sound from heaven as of a rushing mighty wind, and it filled all the house where they were sitting." People who were baptized in the Holy Spirit were completely buried, covered in the Holy Spirit. They were in the house and the whole house was filled with the presence and blessing of the Holy Spirit. That signifies the deep covering of the Holy Spirit of God.

Notice another Scripture. First Corinthians 10 is still another reference to baptism. "And were all baptized unto Moses in the cloud and in the sea" (vs. 2). This was a complete covering. In the cloud—God was overhead. In the sea—two walls on either side. The people of God were on the ground—completely hidden from the unsaved eye. The children of Israel were completely covered when they were "baptized unto Moses" as they crossed the Red Sea. There is not one inference, not one reference, not one implication, not one hint in the Bible that there is any way to be baptized except by immersion.

There is a reason why people have gotten away from that, as they have gotten away from a lot of Bible teaching. There came into being what was called "clinical baptism." By the way, from the day of Pentecost or even from the day of John the Baptist until this very hour, there have always been bodies of believers who baptized by immersion. It never has ceased, not one time, since the days of John the Baptist and the day of Pentecost when baptism was applied to the church. But there is what was called "clinical baptism." Some folks were taught that you got baptized when you got saved. So people said, "When you really get forgiveness of all your sins is when you get baptized. I want to wait until I am closer to death so that when I do get baptized, then all my sins of a lifetime will be forgiven." There has been what you might call "clinical baptism."

Some countries forbid submerging an infant in water not of a proper temperature. Well, infants are not to be baptized anyway. This confusion and other erroneous teaching led to the sprinkling of infants.

"Clinical baptism" means you cannot take a sick person, put him in a body of water and submerge him because it might kill him. So man concocted "clinical baptism," that is, baptizing them on their bed by an affusion, sprinkling or slightly pouring. This is a departure from the Scripture. Nothing is taught like that in the Bible.

V. DOES BAPTISM SAVE?

Let us move on to another question. Is baptism efficacious? Does it save? Don't say to me, "Preacher, you are wasting your time talking about that." You would not believe how many people in the city of Pontiac believe they are saved because they were baptized. They twist the Scriptures to try to make them mean you get saved when you get baptized.

A lady was saved in this church years ago. All of her relatives were in the Church of Christ. This lady came to this church. Neither her loved ones, nor that denomination had ever tried to win her to the Lord. She came to this church and trusted the Lord as her Saviour. She was born again right here in this church one Sunday morning. She said to the folks who brought her, "All my family are members of another church. So, I am going to join the church where my family attends."

Some of the people who helped to win her went and saw her baptized. They heard the preacher say, "My sister So-and-So is being saved tonight by obeying the ordinance of baptism." That was a lie. She was saved before, not when she was baptized! You say, "That's your opinion." Well, it just so happens to be God's opinion, too.

The thief on the cross was saved. We all agree to that. And he was not baptized. Don't let that give you any grounds for saying, "I don't need to be baptized." Listen, it is kind of hard to get baptized when you are nailed to a cross and have only a few minutes more to live. But the thief was saved nevertheless. Jesus said to him, "To day thou shalt be with me in paradise." So he went to Heaven with the Lord unbaptized!

Let us look just quickly at some Scriptures people use to try to teach that you have to be baptized in order to be saved.

Why do some people misinterpret the Scriptures? First, they fail to value the Bible, the Word of God. In II Timothy 2:15 Paul said, "Study to shew thyself approved unto God, a workman that needeth not to be ashamed, rightly dividing the word of truth." He then used an example. He knew some people, Hymenaeus and Philetus, who destroyed the faith of some because they said the resurrection had already passed; it was not future. The Bible says they destroyed the faith of some. I wonder how many more have had their faith shaken and destroyed in the teaching of the Bible because people did not interpret it rightly?

Second, people misinterpret it because they fail to consider other Scriptures. Take II Peter 1:20 which says, "...no prophecy of the scripture is of any private interpretation." Remember that when we get to a Scripture which just looks like it says if you are not baptized, you are not saved. It is not of its own private interpretation. We are to interpret Scripture in the light of the rest of the Bible. People fail to interpret the Scripture because they fail to study the whole Bible.

Some people said to Jesus, "Here's a woman whom seven brothers had as their wife. When one brother died, this one married her," and so forth. (It was perhaps a hypothetical case.) "Seven brothers married her. Seven also died. In the resurrection whose wife shall she be?" You say, "What a foolish question!" Jesus said, "Ye do err, not knowing the scriptures, nor the power of God. For in the resurrection they neither marry nor are given in marriage" (Matt. 12:29, 30). They were foolish because they had not prayerfully studied the Scriptures.

Let us look at some Scriptures now. Mark 16:16 says, "He that believeth and is baptized shall be saved...." The second part says, "...but he that believeth not shall be damned." He that believeth not is lost. It does not say one word about being lost because he is not baptized. "He that believeth and is baptized shall be saved...." So the verse suggests that one could be baptized and still not be saved. It should be interpreted in the light of other Scripture. This is a part of the Great Commission. The Great Commission is given five times, Matthew, Mark, Luke, John and Acts 1. This is the only time there even seems to be a reference to the notion that baptism is essential to salvation. Matthew 28:19 mentions baptism, but admonished us to disciple them first, then baptize them. Win them first, then baptize them.

I make a statement which I think might help. "He that believeth and is baptized shall be saved; but he that believeth not shall be [condemned] damned [lost]."

Suppose I say to Brother Halter tonight, "Now, Brother Halter, he that getteth on the train here in Pontiac and sitteth down shall go to Detroit."

A week later when I see Brother Halter, I say, "Brother Halter, if you get a ticket, get on the train at Pontiac, find you a seat and sit down, you can go to Detroit. He that getteth on the train and sitteth down shall go to Detroit."

A week later I see Brother Halter and I ask, "Brother Halter, did you get on the train and sit down and go to Detroit?"

He says, "Well, I got on the train, but Brother Tom, all of the seats were taken. They have these things like straps you hold onto. I couldn't sit down all the way to Detroit."

I say to him, "Now, where did you go?"

"I went to Detroit."

You see, sitting down was not the main thing. Getting on the train is the main thing.

That is what this verse is like. "He that believeth is saved." That is the main point! Getting baptized is incidental to that. But there is no incidence in the Bible where a person who got saved ever refused baptism. It was just taken for granted. If one believed, he would immediately get baptized. This verse does not teach you have to be baptized in order to be saved. If it did, it would contradict hundreds of other Scriptures which teach salvation is through grace and faith and that alone.

"He that believeth and is baptized shall be saved; but he that believeth not shall be damned." It seems like Paul and James got into an argument. Paul said in Romans 5:1: "Therefore being justified by faith [by faith], we have peace with God...." So Paul said, "You are justified by faith."

James did not say that. He said a man is justified by his works (4:17).

Wait a minute! You mean Paul is saying one thing and James is saying something else? No, they are saying the same thing. Paul is talking about being justified before God. James is talking about proving it before men, justifying your faith before men.

It may be that we can apply that to that verse. When you believe, you are justified before God. When you are baptized, you are saying to men, "I'm a Christian now and justified before men by this work of baptism! I am saying by my water baptism that I have been saved."

Mark 16:16 does not teach that you have to be baptized to be saved.

Let us look at another Scripture, a Scripture that many a person has brought to me and said, "Now this seems to teach something else." I refer to Acts 2:38: "Then Peter said unto them, Repent, and be baptized every one of you in the name of Jesus Christ for the remission of sins, and ye shall receive the gift of the Holy Ghost." People have written me: "You Baptist preachers are preaching falsehood. You don't go far enough. You don't preach all the truth. I'd like to debate you on the radio" (of course, they want me to pay the radio time), or "I'd like to debate you in a public debate." I never fool with them.

Acts 2:38 is really saying, "Then Peter said unto them, Repent, and be baptized every one of you in the name of Jesus Christ BECAUSE of the remission of sins. . . ." It is not in order to get it, but because you already have it. Acts 2:38 does not teach baptismal regeneration.

Acts 2:38 does not teach that baptism is efficacious. I am not a Greek scholar but any Greek student knows that the preposition *eis* which is translated "for" in Acts 2:38 has more than one translation. The preposition is used more than 1700 times in the Greek New Testament. In Matthew 12:41 the preposition is translated "because": "The men of Nineveh shall rise in judgment with this generation, and shall condemn it: BECAUSE they repented at the preaching of Jonas; and, behold, a greater than Jonas is here."

Acts 2:38 is not designed to teach that one gets baptized in order to be saved but "because" of the remission of sins or salvation. We should consider the fact that this verse is spoken in answer to a question. It is not the same question the Philippian jailer asked, "Sirs, what must I do to be saved?" The answer given to him did not even mention baptism. "Believe on the Lord Jesus

Christ, and thou shalt be saved, and thy house" (Acts 16:30, 31). The question that Acts 2:38 answers is, "Men and brethren, what shall we do?" (vs. 37). These convicted Jews were being told to be saved and be baptized as a public testimony that they had believed in the Lord Jesus Christ for the remission of sins.

Why would any honest Christian take an untenable position on Acts 2:38 which would refute dozens of plain Bible verses that teach salvation by faith and grace only?

Let us look at something else. I think it makes it plainer. Peter is preaching on the day of Pentecost. He is trying to prove that Jesus Christ was crucified by these religious leaders. Listen to what he says now, in Acts 2:32, 33:

"This Jesus hath God raised up, whereof we all are witnesses. Therefore being by the right hand of God exalted...."

Now verse 36:

"Therefore let all the house of Israel know assuredly, that God hath made that same Jesus, whom ye have crucified, both Lord and Christ."

He said, "Why, you people killed the Son of God. You killed the true Messiah. You put on a cross God's blessed Son!" They were deeply convicted, says verse 37:

"Now when they heard this, they were pricked in their heart, and said unto Peter and to the rest of the apostles, Men and brethren, what shall we do?"

You see, it is a question. They did not say what the jailer said, "What must I do to be saved?" Rather they said to Peter, "We're guilty! We crucified the wrong man! We've murdered the Son of God!" Under deep conviction they asked, "What shall we do?" Peter answered, "Well, if you mean business, first, repent. To show to all these other unbelieving Jews you are no longer religious but lost, be baptized." "Repent, and be baptized...BECAUSE of the remission of sins, and ye shall receive the gift of the Holy Ghost."

Nowhere in the Bible does it teach that baptism is efficacious. Many verses say, "Believe and be saved," but not one word is mentioned about baptism.

Let me give you one thing and then depart from that and finish.

The Apostle Paul was a great soul winner, was he not? He won many to the Lord, did he not? Listen to what he said in I Corinthians 1:17: "For Christ sent me not to baptize, but to preach the gospel...."

Paul excused himself from baptism. He said on another occasion, 'I baptized the house of Stephanas and maybe one other, I don't remember.' He could not even remember whom he had baptized. Now, somebody has to do it and somebody will, but Paul said, "He didn't send me to baptize." If that is what it took to get people saved, Paul would have had the Mediterranean Sea full of bodies, baptizing everyone he could.

VI. WHY WAS JESUS BAPTIZED?

Matthew 3 gives the plainest account of the baptism of Jesus. Then we will read in Romans 6 just a few verses.

Why was Jesus baptized? He was never unsaved, and Jesus was never saved. Jesus was never unsaved, because Jesus was never lost. He is the divine Son of God. A saved person is one who has confessed his sins. He has been washed from his sins in the blood of Jesus. Jesus was neither unsaved, as you and I, nor was He ever saved, as you and I. He didn't need to be. He was perfect, sinless, without spot; the blessed, eternal Son of God. Why, then, was He baptized?

Matthew 3:13-17:

"Then cometh Jesus from Galilee to Jordan unto John, to be

baptized of him. But John forbad him, saying, I have need to be baptized of thee, and comest thou to me? And Jesus answering said unto him, Suffer it to be so now: for thus it becometh us to fulfil all righteousness. Then he suffered him. And Jesus, when he was baptized, went up straightway out of the water: and, lo, the heavens were opened unto him, and he saw the Spirit of God descending like a dove, and lighting upon him: And lo a voice from heaven, saying, This is my beloved Son, in whom I am well pleased.''

Why did God, on the occasion of the baptism of Jesus, say in an audible voice, "This is my beloved Son, in whom I am well pleased"? We will see that tonight from the Scriptures.

Why was Jesus baptized? I could preach a whole sermon on it. His baptism is mentioned in all four of the Gospels. Take your Bibles and look now at John 1. It answers the reason Jesus was baptized. These words were spoken *after* His baptism.

*"The next day John seeth Jesus coming unto him, and saith, Behold the Lamb of God, which taketh away the sin of the world. This is he of whom I said, After me cometh a man which is preferred before me: for he was before me. And I knew him not [*I did not know who He was at a certain time.]*: but that he should be made manifest to Israel, therefore am I come baptizing with water. And John bare record, saying, I saw the Spirit descending from heaven like a dove, and it abode upon him. And I knew him not: but he that sent me to baptize with water, the same said unto me, Upon whom thou shalt see the Spirit descending, and remaining on him, the same is he which baptizeth with the Holy Ghost. And I saw, and bare record that this is the Son of God.''*—Vss. 29-34.

Why was Jesus baptized? So that He might be presented to people as the Son of God. God said to John, "I'll tell you how you can know it is Jesus when He comes. First, the Holy Ghost will come on Him and remain on Him. Second, God will own Him as His Son in whom He is well pleased." Jesus was baptized that He might present Himself as the Son of God.

He was baptized to say it is not a saving ordinance. He was baptized to show that it pleases God, for God said, "This is my beloved Son in whom I am well pleased" when He was baptized.

He was baptized to set a perfect example (I Peter 2:21). We are to follow in His example. To fulfill all righteousness, that is the Gospel, the death, burial and resurrection of Jesus Christ. That is why Jesus was baptized.

VII. WHAT IF I REFUSE TO BE BAPTIZED?

One might ask, "What if I refuse to be baptized?" It would be a sin: "Therefore to him that knoweth to do good, and doeth it not, to him it is sin" (James 4:16).

A wonderful Christian lady in this room tonight tells of a sister who says she has accepted Christ but will not be baptized. "To him that knoweth to do good, and doeth it not, to him it is sin." To not be baptized is a sin. To refuse means you are not showing friendship to Jesus, who said in John 15:14: "Ye are my friends, if ye do whatsoever I command you." He has told us in His Word that we are to be baptized.

It is not setting a good example. Paul said to young Timothy, ". . . be thou an example of the believers. . ." (I Tim. 4:12).

My wife and our two older children, Joyce and Tommy, spent, a good many years ago, a week in a home where I was holding revival. This was the home of a Baptist preacher whose wife had refused to be baptized. The preacher said to me, "Brother Tom, my wife ought to be baptized. She claims to be saved. I want you to talk with her."

I tried but I couldn't get to first base. She would not accept the Scriptures. She mentioned one or two people she thought were good Christians who had never been baptized. She rebelled against it.

It was impossible to have a revival. We had a meeting, with a few people getting saved, but not a revival. It was impossible to have a revival with that going on.

Several years later that preacher and his wife were divorced. Now he is not even in the ministry. I never met a more sincere man who loved God than that preacher.

Listen! Not to be baptized sets a bad example and it is a sin. It is not being a friend to Jesus. It is not being obedient to the plain teaching of the Word of God.

"What if I'm not baptized?" Well, you could not really say you are not living in sin. You could not call yourself a friend of Jesus. You could not say, "I'm setting a good example." You certainly could not say, "I'm a very good Christian."

You ask, "Will I get to Heaven?" Yes. You will, if you are saved, but you will be miserable every inch of the way. You will be embarrassed when you see that you have not obeyed God. Baptism is for every born-again child of God.

Chapter VI

Officers of the Church

I Timothy 3:1-16

There are so many denominations and so many different religious persuasions because people do not read what the Bible says. The reason there are some religious organizations is because many think the Bible teaching on the organization of the church is something very complicated and very detailed. Such is not the case. In fact, it is very, very simple. Not too many Scriptures deal with the officers of the church.

There are only two officers of the church. We will speak on one tonight, then the other next Wednesday night.

Let me say also that there are officers in this church demanded in the Bible, and some that are not demanded, but neither are they prohibited. The Lord says in His Word, "Let all things be done decently and in order." Some churches feel other officers are necessary other than the two required. The Scripture refers to them as bishops, elders, and one time as pastors. Then the other officer is a deacon.

It would surprise you the questions sometimes people ask about this subject. A few days ago a fine young man, a graduate of a Bible college and a preacher's son, said to me, "Brother Tom, do you think it is all right for a Baptist church to function without deacons?" I said, "Absolutely not." That is one of the two offices that the Bible plainly teaches that ought to be in the church.

I read from I Timothy 3. I praise the Lord for this Book tonight. There are so many false things, so many "isms" in the world. An old preacher one time prayed, "Lord, I'll be glad when all the isms become wasms." I will too. Thank God for a Book that shows us the light and the truth and the way; a Book that teaches us what to believe. Thank God for a perfect Bible, an authoritative Book. I love the Bible. A good man of our church said to me just a few days ago, "Never have I been able to put anything on top of the Bible. I have a Bible on my desk. And I have a Bible at home. But I've never been able to place a stack of mail or another book or a songbook on top of my Bible." Nothing, nothing ought to be between a Christian and his Bible.

I read from I Timothy 3 where much of the teaching about both of these officers of the church is set forth. We will deal just with the one tonight.

"This is a true saying, If a man desire the office of a bishop, he desireth a good work. A bishop then must be blameless, the husband of one wife, vigilant, sober, of good behaviour, given to hospitality, apt to teach; Not given to wine, no striker, not greedy of filthy lucre; but patient, not a brawler, not covetous; One that ruleth well his own house, having his children in subjection with all gravity; (For if a man know not how to rule his own house, how shall he take care of the church of God?) Not a novice, lest being lifted up with pride he fall into the condemnation of the devil. Moreover he must have a good report of them which are without [the unsaved who are outside the church]*; lest he fall into reproach and the snare of the devil. Likewise must the deacons be grave, not doubletongued, not given to much wine, not greedy of filthy lucre; Holding the mystery of the faith in a pure conscience. And let these also first be proved; then let them use the office of a deacon, being found blameless. Even so must their wives be grave,*

not slanderers, sober, faithful in all things. Let the deacons be the husbands of one wife, ruling their children and their own houses well."—Vss. 1-12.

I point this out while reading this passage because I may not remember it next week. The Bible does not say, "If the deacon know not how to rule his own house, how shall he rule the church of God?" It says that about the bishop or pastor.

It does say about the deacon, "Let the deacon be the husband of one wife, ruling his children and his own house well."

I had a deacon once say to me, "Doesn't the Bible say, 'If a man know not how to rule his own house, how shall he rule the church of God'? The deacons are the authority in the church." No, the Bible does not teach that. That deacon read something into the Scripture that is not there. This Scripture deals with bishops and deacons. Now let us finish.

"For they that have used the office of a deacon well purchase to themselves a good degree and great boldness in the faith which is in Christ Jesus. These things write I unto thee, hoping to come unto thee shortly: But if I tarry long, that thou mayest know how thou oughtest to behave thyself in the house of God, which is the church of the living God, the pillar and ground of the truth."— Vss. 13-15.

I. THE SPIRITUAL QUALIFICATIONS OF A PASTOR

I will talk to you about what the Bible, in this particular instance, speaks of as a bishop. We will try to show what "bishop" means. We are talking tonight about the pastor. The word "pastor" is used very slightly in the New Testament and used numerous times in the Old Testament. "Pastor" always has reference to a shepherd. So we are talking tonight about the preacher, the pastor, the man God called to be the shepherd of the sheep. I was thinking while I was putting some things together today, *Oh, how I wish I were a better pastor and a better preacher and a better bishop.* I prayed, "O God, make these things true in my life, these requirements set forth in the Word of God."

When you study about the preacher, the pastor, in the Bible, you will find there is absolutely nothing said about talent as we know the word "talent" and use it today, nothing said about talent in the preacher. I will go you one better than that. There is nothing said in the Bible about a preacher having to be a good and fluent and oratorical preacher in order to be a good pastor and a good shepherd of the sheep. In fact, they said of one of the greatest men of God who ever lived, maybe the greatest, "His bodily presence is weak." Nothing showy about him. And "his speech is contemptible" (II Cor. 10:10), he is not a good speaker, referring to the Apostle Paul.

When people think of preachers, they think he must have some bit of flamboyancy about him. He must have a little bit of charisma. He must have some showmanship. He must be able to speak oratorically, and use beautiful, flowery language. That may be some people's idea of a preacher, but it is not God's teaching about him.

Two words are used which mean practically the same thing in the New Testament. They have reference to the same person. For instance, I read tonight, "If a man desire the office of a bishop, he desireth a good work." The word "bishop" is taken from the Greek word *episkopos.* That is where we get our word "Episcopal." It means "overseer" or "ruler." That word can be used about a man who runs a silver shop and has charge of it. He is the overseer of that shop or store. The word "bishop" means "overseer."

Another word used for the pastor, preacher in the New Testament is the word "elder," which comes from the Greek word *presbuterous.* I suppose that is where we get our word "Presbyterian."

Now "elder" in the New Testament does not refer to chronological age but to spiritual maturity. The "bishop" refers to an overseer. The "elder" refers to spiritual maturity. They both mean one and the same thing. That is, they are not speaking of two people—a bishop and an elder. In fact, the words in some Scriptures are used interchangeably.

Look at it a little further. The word "bishop" is always a proper noun. It refers to a person, while the word "elder" is usually interpreted as an adjective. So we get from that that "bishop" is talking about the man, while "elder" is describing his spiritual maturity. It is a description of a certain kind of spiritual leader.

Now there were elders and bishops in every church in the New Testament. In Acts 14:23 I read where elders and bishops were in every church: "And when they had ordained them elders in every church, and had prayed with fasting, they commended them to the Lord, on whom they believed." So a pastor may be called a "bishop."

The word "bishop" is never in the Bible used as a prelate. It is never used as a man over many, many other preachers. When you see the word "bishop," for instance, as used in the Methodist church, it is not used in a scriptural sense. He is not a prelate. He is an overseer of a flock of born-again people of God. He is the superintendent of the store, so to speak. He is a person who is spiritually mature.

Now he is called a pastor in Ephesians 4, beginning with verse 7. We are going to see something about the pastor, the preacher, as it is set forth in the Bible.

Ephesians 4:7, 8:

"But unto every one of us is given grace according to the measure of the gift of Christ. Wherefore he [Christ] *saith, When he ascended up on high* [His ascension after His death and resurrection], *he led captivity captive, and gave gifts unto men."*

This Scripture is discerned by men of God to be speaking of the moving of the saints from what was Paradise in the lower part of the earth, if you please. You know the story Jesus told. Abraham's bosom was on one side, Paradise. When Jesus died, He descended and He said to the thief, "This day shalt thou be with me in paradise." "When he ascended up on high, he led captivity captive." He liberated, thank God, everyone in Paradise, saved people, and gave gifts unto men. Now look at it:

"(Now that he ascended, what is it but that he also descended first into the lower parts of the earth? He that descended is the same also that ascended up far above all heavens, that he might fill all things.) And he gave some, apostles...."—Vss. 9-11.

The qualification for "apostle" was that they were to have seen with their own physical eyes Jesus Christ in the flesh. So I will ask you, "Is there such a thing tonight?" No, there are no apostles in that sense. Paul calls himself an apostle, for he claimed to have seen Him. He was caught up into Heaven and he saw things and heard words unlawful to utter. He heard Jesus audibly speak. He had seen Christ. He said, "I saw him as one born out of due time." There are no apostles now. Notice: *"...And some, prophets...."*

Prophets in this sense were those who had a special revelation from God, that is, God gave inspired words for those prophets to convey. God is not doing that now. He is not writing any more Bible. I do not think God is even interested in changing the one you and I have before us, let alone writing any more. When you come close to the end of the Bible, we read: "If any man shall add unto these things, God shall add unto him the plagues that are written in this book: And if any man shall take away from the words of the book of this prophecy, God shall take away his part out of the book of life..." (Rev. 22:18, 19). God is not writing any more Bible. We do not believe in progressive revelation. God is not changing any more Bible. I like it like it is. Some folks say,

"Well, folks don't say 'thee' and 'thou' now." So what? Folks don't say a lot of things they used to say, but that does make no difference. I could name a lot of words people used when I was a boy, I mean good words. If I used them here tonight, you would not know what I was talking about.

Suppose I came to you and said, "Have any of you got a poke?" Would you know what I was talking about? No, you would say, "You poke me and I'll poke you!" The country people down South where I was raised used to call a little paper bag a "poke."

So, there are no prophets as such who receive special revelation from God. No man, no woman is getting additional revelation from God. Now watch it:

"...*and some evangelists; and some, pastors....*"

There is very little in the Bible to describe the duties of an evangelist. I thank God for evangelists. I love them and believe in them. I know God has given evangelists as gifts to the church. But there is very little to describe what actually is the duty of an evangelist in the Bible.

"...*and some, pastors and teachers.*"

Now verse 12:

"*For the perfecting* [equipping] *of the saints, for the work of the ministry....*"

What we are doing now is looking at the qualifications and duties of the pastor as set forth in the Word of God. There are many qualifications.

II. HIS RESPONSIBILITIES

1. He is to be a man. "This is a true saying, If a MAN desire the office of a bishop, he desireth a good work."

Hear me out. I do not think God calls women to preach. I have known some fine women preachers. There used to be in our area an evangelistic team of two tremendous women. They were greatly respected. But there is nothing in the Bible that says women are called to preach. "If a man desire the office of a bishop...."

Someone has gone way down deep into the Greek and has said that this verse could be read, "If anyone desire the office of a bishop." But when it discusses this person, it does not say she is to be a woman with one husband, but it does say he is to be a man with one wife. So it is talking about men. He ought to wear his hair like a man. He ought to look masculine. A preacher is to be a man.

A preacher came on the platform not long ago carrying his Bible like a woman carries her purse and taking short steps. I thought, *Lord, I don't want to hear that!* He is to be a man.

2. He is to be above reproach. That does not mean he will be perfect. There are no perfect preachers, no perfect church. Nothing is perfect on this earth. Most churches want a preacher about 30 years of age with about 60 years of experience.

A preacher is to be above reproach. That means that no charge is against him in morality, dishonesty or doctrine.

3. He is to be the husband of one wife. This is not talking about polygamy. It is not talking about a plurality of wives. Paul settled that in Romans 7:2 and I Corinthians 7. Man is to have one wife. A preacher is to be the husband of one wife. This would seem to rule out divorced men being in the ministry.

Now God is tolerant. He sometimes takes all kinds of people and uses them. I used to hear Dr. Bob Jones say, "God's hard up in a sense. He had to use a donkey and a lot of other things. God will take nearly anything He can get, since He wants to use people so badly."

The Bible says, "The husband of one wife." It does not mean if a preacher's wife were to die, he cannot remarry. There is nothing in the Bible that forbids the remarriage of man or woman when their mate has ceased to live. He is to be the husband of one wife. That does not even mean that he has to have a wife. Paul did not have one, and he wrote this letter. He, as far as we know, never had a wife. But, I think it a thing of propriety that preachers have a wife. "Marriage is honourable in all . . ." (Heb. 13:4). He is to be the husband of one wife.

4. He must be vigilant, that is, be on guard against hurting his testimony, against false doctrine and against compromise. He should be on the lookout for his flock, that no false doctrine come in. The very moment a preacher hears certain things in his church, he ought to get them out, like doctors remove cancer from a body, things such as hyper-Calvinism and many other things I could mention. He is to be vigilant. He is to be on the lookout, on his guard, all the time.

5. He must be sober, that is, serious minded. I don't think God meant that a preacher is never to laugh. Good night! If you had to look at what I look at all the time, you couldn't help laughing! Like some of you are laughing now because of what you are seeing! You know what serious minded means. He is not to be flippant, a good-Joe kind of fellow who always has a nice joke ready. The shepherd of the flock should be serious minded, or sober.

6. He must be of good behavior. His conduct and manner of life should be an example to other believers. He should be able to say, as Paul said, "Be ye followers of me, even as I also am of Christ" (I Cor. 11:1).

7. He must be given to hospitality, that is, be friendly and approachable. I have known some preachers in my lifetime who were just the opposite. I am not a good example. I do not even look friendly. I heard someone not long ago talking about it. He said, "You ought to always wear a smile." So I got in front of the mirror and practiced. I put on a smile or two. Listen! I started to get

nauseated. I said, "Now look! I'm going to look like God makes me look because He knows what is inside."

A preacher is to be friendly. He is to be approachable.

I knew a preacher no one could call on the telephone because his number was unlisted. And no one could see him. The brother is dead now. He came to the place where nobody cared whether his number was in the book or not. Nobody cared whether they got a conference with him or not.

I want to say in passing that what is true of a preacher ought to be true of every Christian! Friendly! Given to hospitality.

8. Not only that; he is to be apt to teach. You see that is part of the Great Commission, "...teaching them to observe all things whatsoever I have commanded you." It is my responsibility as pastor to teach the Word of God to my people.

9. "Not given to wine." He is not to be an alcoholic. You say, "Preacher, everybody knows that." No, not everybody. A lot of people do not know that. I could put you in my car and in 20 minutes take you to an institution for alcoholic priests right over near Lake Orion. "Not given to wine."

10. He is not to be greedy. The remedy for greediness is tithes and offerings. If a preacher tithes and gives like he wants his people to, he will not be greedy. "Not greedy of filthy lucre." If a preacher gives liberally to God as he should, it will keep him from being covetous and selfish.

11. He must be patient. Oh, my goodness! When somebody calls you and you are so busy! You have ten minutes to do something that takes thirty minutes to do, and some sweet soul calls and says, "Oh, I was just lonesome and I was thinking of you, Reverend. I thought I'd like to talk to you a little while." You want to say, "Not now." But you have to be patient.

Listen! We had better be afraid not to be patient. Do you know what Romans 5:3 says? "Tribulation worketh patience." So if you are impatient, do not go around bragging about it. "I'm just so nervous. I'm so impatient." The Lord may hit you with something, for "tribulation worketh patience."

12. He must not be a brawler. That is contentious.

13. He must not covet.

14. He must rule his own house well. A preacher's family ought to be saved, won to Christ, living for the Lord. They ought to be with him. He ought to rule his own house well.

15. He must not be a novice, that is, a new convert cannot start out to be a pastor. He should have grown in the Lord and the Word of God before he becomes a pastor. A shepherd ought to know more about God and the Bible than sheep know.

16. He must maintain a good report. He should have a good record and a good testimony.

These are the qualifications and duties of a pastor.

III. THE RESPONSIBILITY OF A PASTOR

1. In the Great Commission in Matthew 28, he is set forth as a baptizer. He is to minister the Lord's Supper. He is to carry out the Great Commission.

2. He is to be a man of prayer. Paul wrote to Timothy, "I exhort therefore, that first of all, supplications, prayers, intercessions, and giving of thanks, be made for all men" (I Tim. 2:1). Every Christian should pray for his President and for our leaders. Some ministers spend nearly their whole ministry running them down. Listen, they are not always good men. The Bible says, "He setteth up whomsoever he will." And God said we are to pray for them. The preacher is to be a man of prayer.

3. That leads me to deacons, appointed in Acts 6. Though the word "deacon" is not found in that chapter, yet there is no question that these seven men who were appointed were deacons. Here is the reason. The apostles, the preachers, the men preaching the

Word of God, said, "It is not reason that we should leave the word of God, and serve tables. Look ye out among you seven men of honest report, full of the Holy Ghost and wisdom whom we may appoint over this business, so we may give ourselves continually to prayer and the ministry of the word" (Acts 6:3, 4). A preacher, a pastor is to give himself to prayer and the ministry of the Word. My, what an important duty!

4. It is the preacher's responsibility to warn people. In this day and time everyone wants you to come out with some beautiful platitudes, make everybody feel good, and say, "Something good is going to happen to you." Don't say anything that might not set well with the people! That is not in the Bible. Somebody said, "You step on my feet." Then move your feet; they are in the wrong place. Preachers are to warn people—I Timothy 4:1: "Now the Spirit speaketh expressly, that in the latter times some shall depart from the faith, giving heed to seducing spirits, and doctrines of devils. . . ." Then verse 6: "If thou put the brethren in remembrance of these things, thou shalt be a good minister of Jesus Christ. . . ." The Bible says we are to warn people!

5. He must live in the Word. I have already alluded to that.

6. He must preach the Bible. If I could just say to you what is on my heart about preaching a social gospel! I know some fundamentalists who are preaching a social gospel. They are more interested in putting bread in somebody's mouth and a coat on his back. Our business is to get God in his soul! The main responsibility of a God-called preacher is, "Preach the word" (II Tim. 4:2)! Not just about it, but preach it!

People have almost had the Bible taken away from them in this country because preachers preach and preach and preach but they do not preach the Bible. I am not putting myself up as a good example, but I have nothing to preach but the Bible. Woe is me if I preach not the Gospel, the Bible.

A preacher must live in the Word and preach the Bible.

7. He must exhort and rebuke—I Thessalonians 5:12: "And we beseech you, brethren, to know them which labour among you, and are over you in the Lord, and admonish you." And Titus 2:5: "These things speak, and exhort, and rebuke with all authority. Let no man despise thee." If you need to rebuke, rebuke! Rebuking is in the Bible just as much as crying, just as much as beseeching, just as much as loving.

Listen! I would not be in the pulpit tonight had I not been rebuked. My grandparents raised me. They are some of the best rebukers I ever had in my life. A preacher is to rebuke when it is necessary. That is not his whole ministry, but he ought to be able to discern when there needs to be rebuke.

8. He is to watch over souls. Let me read you Acts 20:28, a tremendous verse to preachers, to pastors: "Take heed therefore unto yourselves, and to all the flock, over the which the Holy Ghost hath made you overseers, to feed the church of God, which he hath purchased with his own blood." God is saying, "I bought this church with My blood, and I am giving you the responsibility to feed them!" The pastor is to feed the flock of God.

9. He is to be a good example. Paul wrote to Timothy in I Timothy 4:12: "Let no man despise thy youth; but be thou an example of the believers, in word, in conversation, in charity, in spirit, in faith, in purity."

The preacher is to be a good example. A preacher is to tithe his income. A preacher is to pray. A preacher is to win souls. A preacher is to come to church.

Some members of this church are sitting at home watching television right now. Or they are visiting their relatives and staying away from the house of God. When an assembly of God is in session, preachers are to be a good example, and every Christian ought to be also. "Be thou an example. . . ." "Let no man despise thy youth,'' Paul wrote to a man probably 30 years younger than he, ''...but be thou an example of the believers,'' in every way, that is, the preacher.

May God help us to pray for preachers. I covet your prayers that I may be the pastor God wants me to be. More than anything in the world, I want your prayers, your intercession to the throne of grace that I might be a good shepherd of the sheep.

_____ Chapter VII _____

Bible Teaching About Deacons

Philippians 1:1-7

Tonight we are going to talk about deacons in the New Testament church.

I. BACKGROUND TEACHING ON DEACONS

I will refer to a verse, then I read two passages of Scripture that deal with deacons. Let me say this before I even start to read: I doubt if I know of any subject that Christians discuss that is more misunderstood than the matter of deaconship. The Bible is clear on it. But a lot of tradition has crept into the churches about everything, including deaconship. I want us to see what the Bible says. I might also say before I start to read: it is a blessed thing and a tremendous honor to be called a deacon or deaconess, as the Bible also mentions. I might say also that I have never known any better Christian men than the deacons that I have known in my more than 49 years in the ministry.

Philippians 1:1 reads like this: "Paul and Timotheus, the servants of Jesus Christ, to all the saints in Christ Jesus which are at Philippi, with the bishops and deacons." Here you have mentioned in this verse the three constituents, the personal constituents or components of a church. At the church of Philippi which Paul organized, you have saints of God mentioned first; then the bishops or elders, pastors, preachers (the Bible teaches a plurality of preachers wherever it is necessary); then the deacons.

I want to read Acts 6 and I Timothy 3.

The word "deacon" is not found in Acts 6, but there is not a Bible student nor a Bible scholar but what believes Acts 6 is the foundational teaching about deacons in the New Testament church. Let us read Acts 6, then I am going to read a few verses in I Timothy 3.

"And in those days, when the number of the disciples was multiplied. . . . "

The expression, "And in those days," always refers to a period of time which is either passed or in which the personalities are presently engaged.

"And in those days, when the number of the disciples was multiplied, there arose a murmuring of the Grecians against the Hebrews, because their widows were neglected in the daily ministration. Then the twelve called the multitude of the disciples unto them, and said, It is not reason that we should leave the word of God, and serve tables. Wherefore, brethren, look ye out among you seven men of honest report, full of the Holy Ghost and wisdom, whom we may appoint over this business. But we will give ourselves continually to prayer, and to the ministry of the word. And the saying pleased the whole multitude: and they chose Stephen a man full of faith and of the Holy Ghost, and Philip, and Prochorus, and Nicanor, and Timon, and Parmenas, and Nicolas a proselyte of Antioch: Whom they set before the apostles: and when they had prayed, they laid their hands on them. And the word of God increased and the number of the disciples multiplied in Jerusalem greatly; and a great company of the priests were obedient to the faith. And Stephen [one of the deacons], *full of faith and power, did great wonders and miracles among the people. Then there arose*

certain of the synagogue, which is called the synagogue of the Libertines. . . . "

It has been written that when Jesus walked among men in Jerusalem, there were 430 synagogues there and in its environs. Ten people would constitute a congregation in a synagogue. So there were many synagogues. Many bore names of Jews from other countries. So when we read, ''Then there arose certain of the synagogue, which is called the synagogue of the Libertines. . .,'' these were believed to be people who had their citizenship liberty and were Roman citizens, though Jews. Such was Paul.

''. . .Libertines, and Cyrenians, and Alexandrians, and of them of Cilicia and of Asia, disputing with Stephen. And they were not able to resist the wisdom and the spirit by which he spake. Then they suborned men, which said, We have heard him speak blasphemous words against Moses, and against God. And they stirred up the people, and the elders, and the scribes, and came upon him, and caught him, and brought him to the council, and set up false witnesses, which said, This man ceaseth not to speak blasphemous words against this holy place, and the law: For we have heard him say, that this Jesus of Nazareth shall destroy this place, and shall change the customs which Moses delivered us. And all that sat in the council, looking steadfastly on him, saw his face as it had been the face of an angel.''—Vss. 1-15.

Look at a few verses in I Timothy 3. Let us start with verse 8 and read about deacons and deaconesses.

"Likewise must the deacons be grave, not doubletongued, not given to much wine, not greedy of filthy lucre: Holding the mystery of the faith in a pure conscience. And let these also first be proved; then let them use the office of a deacon, being found blameless. Even so must their wives be grave, not slanderers, sober, faithful in all things. Let the deacons be the husband of one wife,

ruling their children and their own houses well. For they that have used the office of a deacon well purchase to themselves a good degree, and great boldness in the faith which is in Christ Jesus."— Vss. 8-13.

II. WHAT THE WORD "DEACON" MEANS

There is a word in the Greek New Testament, *diakonos,* which means "servant" or "minister." That is the word from which we get the word "deacon." Those who deal in ancient languages, especially the Greek and the Hebrew, tell us there is a kindred word, *dioko. Diakonos* is the word from which we get the word "deacon." But there is a kindred word *dioko* also connected with it. These two words have a relationship one to the other. *Dioko* means "to hasten after" or "to pursue," or it can mean "alarm."

One great Bible scholar said, "When you describe a deacon in the New Testament as a servant of God, you are describing one who ministers to the people, one who stirs up the dust because he is busy and a runner on the go for God." A great Bible scholar has said, "A deacon, among other things, was one who literally stirred up the dust," meaning he is busy at the work of the Lord.

III. HISTORY OF THE CHURCH AT PHILIPPI

You are familiar with this church at Philippi which Paul organized or founded. I gave you one verse mentioning the saints of God, the preachers and deacons in the church at Philippi. When Paul went to Philippi, the chief city of Macedonia, he first met Lydia, a great and religious woman who conducted religious meetings, prayer meetings. But the Bible says that "the Lord opened her heart." She became a real Christian.

Paul and Silas walked along the street and a demonic young woman, used by men to tell fortunes, etc., followed after them. She was a slave of evil men. Recognizing Paul and Silas as men of God, she said, "These men are servants of the most high God. I'm a servant of evil." She too believed and was saved.

Paul and Silas were put into jail, as you well know. At midnight the earthquake came. God heard their singing and their praying and delivered them after the midnight hour. They went to the jailer's home, who washed their stripes. That night he believed with all of his house and was baptized.

So there was born in Philippi what we call a New Testament church, made up of a body of baptized believers.

IV. DEACONS ARE REQUIRED IN THE NEW TESTAMENT CHURCH

When Paul organized that church, there was in that church the preachers and the deacons. It is a pattern for New Testament churches. I mentioned to you that someone asked me recently, "Can you have a New Testament Baptist church and not have deacons?" I said, "No." An attorney said to me, "The church where I have been attending has placed on the Board a man who divorced his first wife and married another. He is now a deacon in the church. Pastor, can that man be a deacon?" I said, "Absolutely not."

The Bible speaks plainly about the requirements of a deacon.

The first Christian martyr, the very first man in the New Testament days who literally laid down his life as a witness for Jesus Christ was none other than a deacon of a New Testament church, Deacon Stephen. There was never a more godly man. Just before he died, Stephen saw the Son of God standing on the right hand of God. He knew about how Jesus had died, and he wanted to die like a Christian ought to die. He remembered that when Jesus died on the cross of Calvary, He said, "Father, into thy hands I commend my spirit." So when Stephen died, this great deacon, he said, "Lord Jesus, receive my spirit." He remembered that, when Jesus died upon the cross of Calvary, robed in blood and crowned with thorns, He had prayed, "Father, forgive them, for they know not what they do." So when Stephen died, he not only said, "Lord Jesus, receive my spirit," but he prayed to Jesus at the throne of God in Heaven, "Lay not this sin to their charge."

So the first Christian martyr in the New Testament day was a deacon.

The first great individual soul winner in the New Testament and in the Book of Acts and in the early church days was a deacon by the name of Philip. We read in Acts 8:5 that he went to the godless city of Samaria and preached Christ unto them. Then the Holy Spirit attached him to a chariot of the Ethiopian eunuch. Verse 35 says, "Philip opened his mouth, and began at the same scripture, and preached unto him Jesus."

The first Christian martyr in the New Testament was a deacon. The first great soul winner in the Church Age was a deacon out of this New Testament church at Jerusalem.

This office is important. There are many offices in the church which are good. "Let all things be done decently and in order" (I Cor. 14:40). It is good to have people handle certain things, custodians of the properties and holdings of real estate, those who deal with finance and money, those who have offices in music, teaching and other things. Many of these are not demanded in the Bible. But the office of a deacon is absolutely demanded in the Bible.

I want you to think about this. Three whole chapters in the Book of Acts deal with deacons. In chapter 6, they are elected and appointed. In chapter 7, we read probably the longest recorded sermon other than the Sermon on the Mount. It was preached by Deacon Stephen. In chapter 8, we read of a revival and soul winning and the miraculous work of God under the minstry of a deacon, Philip. So here are three chapters God put right in the Book of Acts which deal with the deaconship and especially the ministry of two of them.

I could stand here tonight and tell how deacons have touched my life. I shall never cease to thank God for a Baptist deacon by the name of Earl Clemons. I met Earl before I became a Baptist pastor. He touched my life as much as any man I have ever known, maybe with the exception of Dr. Bob Jones, Sr. Earl Clemons was a man of God. You could see Jesus in his countenance and hear Jesus speak in his words. You could feel Jesus loving you through his life. I loved Earl Clemons, a Baptist deacon.

I shall never cease to thank God for some deacons I have known in this church. I remember a Saturday night many, many long years ago when I preached in a little church over here in a week of revival. On a Saturday night when the invitation was given, several people came to be saved. One was Ralston Calvert. Ralston became a Baptist deacon.

On the other side of the altar came a long, straight, lean man. He knelt that night and wept. He gave his heart to Jesus Christ. That man was Freeman Johnson. For 25 years Freeman lived a life above reproach. He served as a deacon in this church, then moved to another state. Freeman Johnson was a man of few words. His just saying, "Um hummm" would influence the whole board meeting! Or his "Uh uh" would have tremendous influence on the whole meeting.

I think about Brother Wally Swanson. God only knows what this church as a body of believers owes to the life and ministry of Wally Swanson. A pastor never had a better friend and a church never knew a better deacon. I know people tonight in the ministry who will tell you that Wally Swanson led them to the Lord. I know others who have come down these aisles to be saved who will tell you, "I never will forget when that deacon, Brother Wally

Swanson, showed me from the Bible how to be saved.''

So the Bible demands the office of a deacon.

V. THE DUTIES OF A DEACON

There are three great explanatory words in Acts 6:1 and all begin with an ''m''; *multiplied, murmuring* and *ministration.*

We could take these three words and give you the history of why deacons came into being.

In the early New Testament church there was, first of all, the multiplied believers. Three thousand had been saved on the day of Pentecost. The number rose to 5,000. Then we read there were 4,000 men. Then we read there was a multitude of believers. Then we read there were ''multitudes'' of believers, both men and women. So the Lord was saving thousands of people. The number of Christians was being multiplied.

Keep in mind that in chapter 2 of the Book of Acts, about sixteen nationalities of Jews were mentioned. Jews who had been scattered over the face of the earth came to Jerusalem for the week of Pentecost and were there on the day of Pentecost from all of these different nations. These were called Grecian Jews or Hellenistic Jews because they spoke the Greek language and used the Greek Scriptures. There were thousands of them in Jerusalem, with their wives. So great sums of money had been given. Here are all these thousands who had come from sixteen different countries at least. They hear such revival, such blessing of God, such outpouring from Heaven, that they do not even pretend to leave immediately to go back home. They might have stayed a year, and some may never have returned to where they were born.

One day Barnabas sold his land and gave it to the church. These people, with no permanent home, no job, must be taken care of. So there arose a murmuring. These Hellenistic Jews, these Grecians, as they are called here, these foreign-born Jews, complained.

"Now our widows are not getting a fair share at the tables where the food is dispensed, and the money is used that has been given in great sums, like that which Barnabas gave." So there was a murmuring about the ministration of the food and dealing at the tables as these people were being taken care of.

It also mentions here the Hebrews. These Hebrews were natives of the land of Palestine, native born. They spoke not the Greek but the Hebrew language and dealt in the Hebrew Scriptures. So here are both Jews, thousands of each group, but there is quite a bit of difference between them even though they were Christians. Why, the native-born Jews said, "The Temple is ours. Pentecost came here in this great temple yard and around here where we've been serving the Lord and worshiping all these years." So, a problem arose.

This thing necessitated a church meeting. The twelve apostles who were organized and were organizing said to the multitude, "You pick you out seven men whom we may appoint over this business." Thus we have the agelong practice in Baptist churches that people have the greater part in the selection of deacons. The twelve apostles said, "You pick out seven men, seven men with certain characteristics whom we may appoint over this business," that is, this administration of food and perhaps of money, taking care of hoards and multitudes who were homeless and jobless. So, it necessitated a church meeting.

The people and the disciples had a part in the election of the deacons.

Now here is one of the most beautiful things you can read of in the Bible. People talk about deacons and trouble, and God knows there are Baptist churches where there is much trouble, but it is not always the fault of deacons. It is many times the fault of us preachers. Here was a problem, but notice the wonderful way in which it was settled, in Acts 6. These twelve said, "Now you pick out seven men. You Hellenistic Jews, you foreign-born Jews, you are the ones who have been complaining. This is a problem that you've brought to our attention. Now, out of this multitude of both groups of Jews, you pick out seven men.''

So they were picked out and elected. All seven of the first deacon board were elected from the Hellenistic Jews. All seven of these deacons were elected from the group who had come from other places, but now are here in this early church and making that locality their home. They settled it in love, without a loss, without a heartache. The early deacon board was born in one of the greatest acts of love you will ever find in the Bible.

They elected seven deacons. For many years Baptist churches used to say, ''Every Baptist church ought to have seven deacons.'' It does not really make that much difference. Some churches did not have seven members when they started, and some churches do not have seven qualified men a year or two later. There may be churches many years old that do not have seven men who meet the requirements.

I do not know why ''seven deacons,'' except seven is a tremendous number in the Bible. There is what is called a ''hebdomad'' that is, seven days make a week. The Bible practically opens with that. The Passover Feast went on for seven days. A male child had to live for seven days before he could be circumcised on the eighth day. Seven times seven years brought the year of Jubilee. Seven churches, seven plagues.

They elected seven deacons. I am one student of the Bible who believes that the number seven is really not significant in this instance. There is no teaching to that effect.

VI. QUALIFICATIONS OF DEACONS

Let us look at the qualifications of these deacons. Acts 6 says, ''Look ye out among you seven men of honest report,'' men with no charge standing against them, men of a good testimony. These seven deacons had to be men "full of the Holy Ghost." Deacons are commanded to be Spirit-filled as much as a preacher or anyone else. They were to be men of "wisdom," men who knew how to deal with matters, men who could wisely apply themselves to the solution of problems. James 1:5 says, "If any of you lack wisdom, let him ask of God that giveth to all men liberally . . . ." They must be men who have wisdom from God.

Many Baptist churches have put men on deacon boards just because they were "professional." Or put them on a board because they had an education. None of us are enemies to education. None of us are enemies to a person having a lofty profession. But these are to be men of heavenly wisdom, these deacons! Men of honest report, full of the Holy Ghost, full of wisdom, full of faith, as verse 3 of Acts 6 says. It implicates beyond any shadow of a doubt that they were to be soul winners.

Notice what Stephen, this deacon, did immediately. Acts 6:8: "And Stephen, full of faith and power, did great wonders and miracles among the people." What is the power for? Acts 1:8: "Ye shall receive power after that the Holy Ghost is come upon you: and ye shall be witnesses unto me . . . ." These deacons were expected to be soul winners.

They were to have spiritual boldness. Notice Acts 6:10: "And they were not able to resist the wisdom and the spirit by which he [Stephen] spake." He was bold for the Lord! Not a foolish person who just paraded religion; but one who was bold to speak for Jesus Christ. That was Stephen. A deacon was expected to have spiritual boldness like Peter and John had. Acts 4:13: "Now when they saw the boldness of Peter and John . . . they took knowledge of them, that they had been with Jesus"—when they had seen their boldness. So a deacon was to be bold in spiritual matters, bold in the Word of God.

The next qualification I find in Acts 6 is that these deacons were to be men of a good countenance. Deacon Stephen looked like a Christian. Acts 6:15: "And all that sat in the council, looking stedfastly on him, saw his face as it had been the face of an angel."

Do you know what makes a person's countenance look right? Fellowship with God! When Moses went with the Lord 40 days and nights, he came out and his face shone. He, humbly, was not conscious of the fact, but the people knew it. Stephen looked like a man of God. He attired himself, he expressed himself as a man of God. The look upon his face, his countenance, was that of a person of God.

In I Timothy 3:8, there are several other qualifications. These overlap a little, yet not completely.

It says deacons are to be grave, that is, not a "sour puss." You know, folks get the wrong idea: "If you are a Christian, don't ever laugh! It is not spiritual!" Sometimes those trying to look spiritual go around looking real pious and green and sickly. There is no spirituality in that! I'm enjoying being a Christian so much that sometimes I nearly laugh out loud! I thank God I am not going to Hell. I am happy. And if you are not, you had better get happy. This Bible speaks of joy, joy, joy! peace, peace, peace! Quit being a sour puss. There is no spirituality in trying to see how mean you can look. "Grave" means "serious minded, not frivolous."

Now notice, "not doubletongued." In the Bible that means two things: say one thing and mean another; or say one thing to this person and something else to the other person. "Not doubletongued."

"Not greedy." Why does it say that? Here are some people who are going to handle large sums of money. Barnabas, having lands, sold it and gave all he had. Ananias and Sapphira gave probably quite a bit, but they lied about it and the Lord took them to

Heaven prematurely. God said in His Word that a deacon is not to be greedy.

There were religious leaders in the Bible who were just the opposite. Think of Balaam. He ruined himself thinking about what he could get. I think of Gehazi. When Elisha spoke to the general of the Syrian army, Naaman, Naaman said, "I have been healed and I'm so thankful. Let me give you something." Elisha said, "No," knowing that if he let him give him something because of the mercy and grace of God bestowed upon him, he would have always thought he had helped pay for what had happened to him. So he refused it.

Gehazi, hearing all of this, ran after Naaman when he was going home and said, "My master Elisha has changed his mind. We've had company come and we need some clothes and food. Elisha's decided he will take it." That was a lie. What happened? Gehazi became a leper and was one the rest of his life. God judges greedy people in the Lord's work.

I think of Judas Iscariot. Judas wanted 30 pieces of silver so badly that he sold our Lord for it. He was an elected official. He was elected over the treasury of the Apostolate. This is something all of us should heed: Do not be greedy.

Do you know the greatest remedy in the world for greediness? Giving. Tithe your income. Give to God. Then you will not be greedy because you will say, "The more I make, the more I can give to the Lord. To God be the glory!" The preacher will shout, "Hallelujah! We can pay our debts and be honorable!" Be not greedy.

I have had millions of dollars go through my hands. I thank God I can look Him in the face and say, "I never took a dollar of God's money in my life."

Did you know some folks steal from God every Sunday? Some steal their own tithe from God. I've even heard of those who would steal somebody else's tithe. I would be afraid God would kill me. If I didn't tithe my own income, it would scare me to death. Any Christian ought to be scared.

Deacons are to be liberal with God.

They are to be lovers of the Scriptures, holding the faith in a pure conscience. Stephen and Philip knew the Bible, did they not? Stephen preached his sermon in Acts 7, and it is a resumé of the whole Old Testament. And he knew it by heart. Philip certainly knew the Scriptures. "He began at the same scripture and preached unto him Jesus" (Acts 8:35).

They are to use their office well. They are to be peacemakers and helpers. They are not to be a novice, not a brand new convert. A deacon is to be the husband of one wife with a disciplined family and a miniature church in his own home.

Thus the teaching of the Bible about deacons.

Chapter VIII

The Orders Given to the Church

Luke 24:47

If you and I could sit down and talk for ten minutes, what would be my opinion as to what was closest to your heart? And what would you say was closest to the heart of Brother Tom?

Jesus left no doubt about what was closest to His heart.

I will speak from five Scriptures.

"And as they thus spake, Jesus himself stood in the midst of them, and saith unto them, Peace be unto you. But they were terrified and affrighted, and supposed that they had seen a spirit. And he said to them, Why are ye troubled? and why do thoughts arise in your hearts? Behold my hands and my feet, that it is I myself: handle me, and see: for a spirit hath not flesh and bones, as ye see me have. And when he had thus spoken, he shewed them his hands and his feet. And while they yet believed not for joy, and wondered, he said unto them, Have ye here any meat? And they gave him a piece of a broiled fish, and a piece of an honeycomb. And he took it, and did eat before them. And he said unto them, These are the words which I spake unto you, while I was yet with you, that all things must be fulfilled which were written in the law of Moses, and in the prophets, and in the psalms, con-

cerning me. Then opened he their understanding, that they might understand the scriptures, and said unto them, Thus it is written, and thus it behooved Christ to suffer, and to rise from the dead the third day: And that repentance and remission of sins should be preached in his name among all nations, beginning at Jerusalem. And ye are witnesses of these things. And, behold, I send the promise of my Father upon you: but tarry ye in the city of Jerusalem, until ye be endued with power from on high. And he led them out as far as to Bethany, and he lifted up his hands, and blessed them. And it came to pass, while he blessed them, he was parted from them, and carried up into heaven. And they worshipped him and returned to Jerusalem with great joy: and were continually in the temple, praising and blessing God.''—Luke 24:36-53.

For our text notice verse 47: ''. . .that repentance and remission of sins should be preached in his name among all nations, beginning at Jerusalem.''

Five times in the first five books of the New Testament we have recorded, by four different writers, what is called the Great Commission.

Jesus Christ has given a commission to the church. If you want to know what is closest to the heart of the Lord Jesus Christ, you notice the five times that the Great Commission is given in the first five books of the New Testament. The thing closest to His heart is soul winning, seeing people saved, seeing people hear about Jesus, who can satisfy the longing of the heart, forgive sin and save people from sin.

Wherever you find Jesus in the Bible, He is interested in someone's soul.

You see Him sitting at Jacob's Well, in John 4, thirsty and tired, but there is a longing in His heart that supersedes His desire for water and rest. There comes a lost woman. Jesus talks with her and leads her to Christ. The disciples come later with food to eat, but He tells them, "I have meat to eat that ye know not of" (John 4:32).

The thing closest to the heart of Jesus Christ is to see people saved. This is the thing for which He came into the world. "The Son of man is come to seek and to save that which was lost" (Luke 19:10).

Five times in the first five books of the New Testament Jesus gives the commission to the church. Every church, every church member, every preacher, every Christian ought to be interested in knowing what that commission to the church is. Before He left this world, what did the Lord Jesus Christ tell the church that its job was? What is the thing that, five times, Jesus talked about just before the heavens burst with the glory of God and Jesus was received out of sight?

I. PROMISE OF HIS PRESENCE
Matthew 28:20

Notice in the closing verses of the Gospel of Matthew, we find for the first time in the New Testament, the commission of the Lord Jesus Christ to the church.

"All power is given unto me in heaven and in earth. Go ye therefore, and teach all nations, baptizing them in the name of the Father, and of the Son, and of the Holy Ghost: Teaching them to observe all things whatsoever I have commanded you: and, lo, I am with you alway, even unto the end of the world."—Matt. 28:18-20.

Each of these five times He makes a separate and distinct promise to the church or to the Christian who will win lost souls: 'If you carry out my commission, you can depend on my presence.'

Each of these five times He guarantees the Christian something; every one of the times He assures the Christian of something different, if he would be a soul winner.

Here He says, 'If you go into all the world, if you make the Gospel known, if you put soul winning first in your church, heart, life and time, "Lo, I am with you alway, even unto the end of the world." '

There is a sense in which He is with each Christian, even if he never lifts his hand to win a soul. There is a sense in which God is with me if I never speak to another lost soul from now until my dying day. Since Jesus came into my heart 41 years ago, He has never forsaken me, no never. God Almighty is with me all the time.

But here is something special: Jesus said, "If you go into all the world. . . ." Your world starts right where you are. It starts on your street, in your office, wherever you touch one human life. Jesus said, "If you go to people with the Gospel, lo, I am with you alway, even unto the end of the age."

I think of some of the wonderful moments of my fellowship with the Lord Jesus Christ—and I have enjoyed some wonderful moments. When I go into my office, close the door, get down on my knees, with God's Book open before me, and ask Him to speak to me and then tell Him what I have on my heart, that is a wonderful moment!

It is a wonderful moment when every night before bedtime I take the Word of God, gather my family about me, and read a chapter of God's Holy Word; we bow our heads and thank God for His goodness upon our home and family. That is a wonderful moment when I feel God is with us as we pray.

But only one time has the Lord promised His presence in a special way to a Christian and that is when a Christian is in the act of soul winning. "If you go," He said, "lo, I am with you alway, even unto the end of the age."

It's a mystery to me why it is so hard to get people to do what Jesus says we are supposed to do—that is, witness to the lost. Never am I more conscious of His presence than when I am out to win a soul to Him.

II. PROMISE OF HIS PROTECTION
Mark 16:15-18

In the Book of Mark, Jesus gives the Great Commission with the promise of His protection. Notice the five things that Jesus promises His disciples:

1. They could cast out devils.
2. They could speak with new tongues, or new languages.
3. They could take up serpents.
4. If they drank any deadly thing, it would not hurt them.
5. They were to have victory over disease.

I have often given thought and prayer to this passage because there are some difficulties attached. There are two or three things I believe to be true concerning this passage which ought to be considered here.

First, from verse 9 to verse 20 there is a question in the minds of some people about its inspiration. Scofield footnotes make plain these verses are not found in the two oldest and most authoritative manuscripts, the Sinaitic and the Vatican. Nevertheless, it was quoted, as we have it, by the early church saints, and soon after Pentecost, and without a doubt as a part of the sacred writings inspired of God.

A second matter that should be mentioned is this: this particular Scripture might be said to be abstract in nature. The signs Jesus gave here, which were to follow preaching the Gospel and winning the lost, were definitely abstract. The apostles had these signs in their ministry. For instance, on the island of Malta, Paul was bitten by a venomous serpent, which did him no harm because God was with him to protect him. His work was not completed, and until the work of soul winning was finished, God would allow no harm to come to him.

The third thing, and to me the most wonderful, is this: beyond any doubt the passage is designed to teach God's special protection and that the angels of the Lord encamp around about those who seek to do His will and send His Word to the ends of the earth. I have the assurance in my heart that no evil could possibly befall me as I seek to win the lost, except it come from the hand of God as a part of His directive will for my life and ministry.

I know that many of God's chosen saints have laid down their lives for the Gospel's sake, have been torn asunder, thrown to the wild beasts and burned at the stake. But I believe that by the cruel persecution and death of these saints of God they have won more people and sent the Gospel further into the regions of the world than they ever could have by living.

God protects His soul winners. Thank God for this! If you will consecrate your services this day to the Lord and put soul winning first in your life, now and forever, God's hand will be on you in a most wonderful and special way. I have been in places myself, where, had it not been for His assisting grace and His overcoming power, I do not believe I could have come out unscathed and unharmed.

III. PROMISE OF HIS PROGRAM

Luke 24:46, 47

In the Book of Luke, Jesus outlines His program in the Great Commission:

"Thus it is written, and thus it behooved Christ to suffer, and to rise from the dead the third day; And that repentance and remission of sins should be preached in his name among all nations BEGINNING AT JERUSALEM."—Luke 24:46, 47.

Jesus said, "The Gospel must go to the ends of the earth." But where is this church to start? Where are you twelve disciples to begin? Where are you to start? Jesus said, "...among all nations [but] BEGINNING AT JERUSALEM."

Why? It was at Jerusalem where wicked people crucified the Son of God, and they were as lost as the heathen in the darkest part of the world. Jesus is teaching here that before you can send the Gospel to Africa and India, you must evangelize at home. And that is the program for this church and for any New Testament Christian church. The biggest farce in the world is to send a dollar to Africa and not knock on a door in Pontiac. It is hypocrisy and mockery!

Why do not some people win souls at home? Perhaps they have never seen the truth that Jesus taught—to start at Jerusalem. It means start with yourself. Be sure that you are saved. Be sure you know Christ as your own personal Saviour. Start at Jerusalem. That is where you are to start winning souls.

The program of our church is to make Christ known by radio, by preaching, by paper, by house-to-house visitation, by word of mouth—every way we possibly can. That was also the program of the early church. That was the program of the church at Pentecost. That was the program of the church filled with the Holy Ghost. "Daily in the temple, and in every house, they ceased not to teach and preach Jesus Christ" (Acts 5:42).

Many church members criticize the soul-winning program, criticize the preacher who preaches the Gospel, when the only thing they need is an old-fashioned dose of salvation, repentance of sin and getting right with God.

The program of Jesus is soul winning, and if we do not put that first, we cannot do anything right for God. The biggest mockery in the world is to have a Christian school in a church that does not win souls. The biggest mockery on earth is to have a seminary in a church that is not winning people to Christ.

I expect every board member of my church to have a part in

soul winning. Any member of the board who wouldn't help win souls to Jesus Christ is not worthy of the position.

I wouldn't give you a nickel for a choir member who sings, "Oh, How I Love Jesus," and fights a program which promotes the Gospel.

I wouldn't give you a nickel for a Sunday school teacher who has no interest in knocking on doors and telling people about Jesus and trying to get people to trust the Lord.

It is a hypocritical farce for a person to be a choir member, board member, or Sunday school teacher and have no interest in the souls of lost men and women.

Isn't it strange that that which was closest to the heart of Jesus, is furthest from the heart of the average Christian? Do you understand how it could be, that the thing closest to Jesus' heart, so often is furthest from the hearts of so-called professing people of God? I wonder sometimes if the reason is because the person has not started at Jerusalem. I believe that every genuine, born-again Christian has the desire to win the lost to Christ.

I read a story of a poor young girl from the slums of London who knocked on the door of an educated and refined English preacher and said, "I want you to get my mother in."

This preacher said, "If your mother is out, that is no concern of mine. I can't get her in. You will have to get her in the best way you can."

"But," she persisted, "you don't understand. You're a preacher, and my mother is dying and she isn't in, and I want you to get her in. Don't you see? It's Heaven I want my mother in."

This preacher, a modernist, and interested in his salary, in remarks people made about him and his reputation, said, "I don't know whether I can help you or not, but I'll go with you."

This poor urchin from the slums led the brilliant, modernistic, unsaved man to the little old hovel where her mother was dying.

The preacher went in and sat down in a dirty chair while the girl stood by the bed. He looked at the dying woman.

The girl said, "Now, preacher, you get her in."

He commenced talking to her about the age of the earth.

But the old lady said, "I don't want to hear about the age of the earth. I want to hear something about the Rock of Ages."

The preacher said, "Well, I don't know what to say to you, but I'll read you something if you have a Bible."

The girl brought the old Book. He read John 3:16, "For God so loved the world, that he gave his only begotten Son, that whosoever believeth in him should not perish, but have everlasting life."

A smile came on the old lady's face as she said, "I'm in, preacher! I'm in!"

In a moment she died and she went to Heaven.

The preacher bowed his head and said to the woman's daughter. "Yes, and thank God, I'm in too! While I was getting your mother in, I got in, too. I've been saved here tonight."

Listen friend, if you're not interested in getting somebody out of Hell and into Heaven, I would wonder if you have really been saved.

IV. PROMISE OF HIS PEACE
John 20:19-21

The fourth time the Great Commission is given is in John. Here Jesus guaranteed something else to the soul winner.

In John 20:19-21, the Great Commission is given in another form:

"Then the same day at evening, the first day of the week, when the doors were shut where the disciples were assembled for fear of the Jews, came Jesus and stood in the midst, and saith unto them, Peace be unto you. And when he had so said, he shewed

unto them his hands and his side. Then were the disciples glad, when they saw the Lord. Then said Jesus to them again, Peace be unto you: as my Father hath sent me, even so send I you.''

Jesus said, ''As you go out telling that commission, giving that Gospel, you will have great peace in your own life.''

We talk about warped and twisted personalities; the only thing wrong with some personalities is that people are not doing the will of God. The greatest adjustment in human life is to be in God's will and to be doing what He wants done. That will adjust more

• personalities than anything else. The greatest peace that can ever come into the heart of a human being is the peace of knowing you have done your best, as a Christian, to see people saved.

A few years ago someone sent me a message to go see a man in the hospital. I went to see him three times. The first time, I could get nowhere. But I knew that man was lost and sick.

I went back the second time and stood by his bed. He did not want to hear it, but since God had given me the responsibility to tell it, I stood at the bedside and read John 3:16, Acts 16:31 and told him the wonderful plan of salvation. He didn't get saved. I thought, *O God, when I walk out of this hospital, I want to be able to say that man on his dying bed heard the Gospel. And when I stand before the throne of God, I don't want the blood of that man's soul to be on my hands.*

Later I received a message that he was worse, so I went back the third time. I said, ''Friend, can you hear me?''

''Yes.''

''Can you understand what I am saying?''

''Yes.''

I went over the plan of salvation again. I bowed my head and prayed. His eyes, I believe, were wide open. I don't think he showed any interest.

Then, one day the message came, ''He's dead.''

His destiny is forever sealed. Never will he hear the Gospel again.

When the death message came, I said to my wife, "Honey, thank God, I did my best."

Friend, death and disaster strike everywhere. It is happening to your neighbors, your friends, your loved ones. How will it be when the doctor says, "Your daddy is dying"? or, "Your sister is dead"? Can you lift your voice toward Heaven and say, "God, I did my best; I put You first in my life, my heart, my home, my business. I tried to make You known to some lost soul"?

V. PROMISE OF HIS POWER

Acts 1:8

Jesus guarantees us His power. The fifth time the Great Commission is given is in Acts 1:8:

"But ye shall receive power, after that the Holy Ghost is come upon you; and ye shall be witnesses unto me in Jerusalem, and in all Judaea, and in Samaria, and unto the uttermost part of the earth."

You say, "Brother Tom, I want to win souls but I can't. I'm not strong enough." Neither am I. But Jesus guarantees His power. He said that you can have the power of the Holy Ghost to win souls. Every man, every woman who wants to see people saved, who wants to evangelize this city and send the Gospel to the ends of the earth, can have the power of God to do it—that is, if you want that power.

How about it, friend? Are you saved? Are you interested in making the Gospel known? That is the thing closest to the heart of Jesus. That is on my heart. That is what you are going to hear every time a sermon is preached from my pulpit. It is the commission to the church. The Captain of the church says, "These are My orders."

God give us men and women who will say, "As for me, dear Jesus, I am ready. I will take Your Gospel wherever You want it to go. I'll be a humble, faithful witness for You."

This is the message God gave me to give you.

Chapter IX

The Stewardship of the Church

Luke 12:42-48   Matthew 25:14-30

After I read the Scripture, you will know a little more what we are talking about when we say, "The Stewardship of the Church." Turn to Luke 12:42-48. I will read a part of what is called the parable of the steward and the servants. Then I will turn to another part of the Word of God, Matthew 25:14-30.

Luke 12:42-48:

"And the Lord said, Who then is that faithful and wise steward, whom his lord shall make ruler over his household, to give them their portion of meat in due season? Blessed is that servant, whom his lord when he cometh shall find so doing. Of a truth I say unto you, that he will make him ruler over all that he hath. But and if that servant say in his heart, My lord delayeth his coming...."

I have the strongest feeling tonight that this is what many are saying about the coming of the Lord: "My lord delayeth his coming...." He has delayed it. I believe the coming of the Lord is imminent, that is, it could take place momentarily. The Lord could come while you and I are sitting in this service. I do not believe there is one prophecy yet to be fulfilled before the Lord could come. This parable says:

"But and if that servant say in his heart, My lord delayeth his

coming; and shall begin to beat the menservants and maidens, and to eat and drink, and to be drunken; The lord of that servant will come in a day when he looketh not for him, and at an hour when he is not aware, and will cut him in sunder and will appoint him his portion with the unbelievers. And that servant, which knew his lord's will, and prepared not himself, neither did according to his will, shall be beaten with many stripes. But he that knew not, and did commit things worthy of stripes, shall be beaten with few stripes. For unto whomsoever much is given, of him shall be much required: and to whom men have committed much, of him they will ask the more.''

Turn to Matthew 25. We are getting to the subject we call ''The Stewardship of the Church.'' By the way, I think there are some 38 parables told by our Lord, and more than a dozen have to do with stewardship, or what to do with what God has put in our care and keeping.

Matthew 25:14-30:

''For the kingdom of heaven is as a man travelling into a far country, who called his own servants, and delivered unto them his goods. And unto one he gave five talents, to another two, and to another one; to every man according to his several ability; and straightway took his journey. Then he that had received the five talents went and traded with the same, and made them other five talents. And likewise he that had received two, he also gained other two. But he that had received one went and digged in the earth, and hid his lord's money. After a long time the lord of those servants cometh, and reckoneth with them.''

Verse 19 seemed to stand out to me: ''After a long time the lord of those servants cometh, and reckoneth with them.'' It does seem like a long time. Two thousand years ago He said, ''And if I go and prepare a place for you, I will come again, and receive you unto myself. . . ." Our loved ones have come and gone. The years have come and gone. It does seem like a long time.

"After a long time the Lord of those servants cometh, and reckoneth with them. And so he that had received five talents came and brought other five talents, saying, Lord, thou deliveredst unto me five talents: behold I have gained beside them five talents more. His lord said unto him, Well done, thou good and faithful servant: thou hast been faithful over a few things, I will make thee ruler over many things: enter thou into the joy of thy lord. He also that had received two talents came and said, Lord, thou deliverest unto me two talents: behold, I have gained two other talents beside them. His lord said unto him, Well done, good and faithful servant; thou hast been faithful over a few things, I will make thee ruler over many things: enter thou into the joy of thy lord. Then he which had received one talent came and said, Lord, I knew thee that thou art an hard man, reaping where thou hast not sown, and gathering where thou hast not strawed: And I was afraid, and went and hid thy talent in the earth; lo, there thou hast that is thine. His lord answered and said unto him, Thou wicked and slothful servant, thou knewest that I reap where I sowed not, and gather where I have not strawed: Thou oughtest therefore to have put my money to the exchangers, and then at my coming I should have received mine own with usury. Take therefore the talent from him, and give it unto him which hath ten talents. For unto every one that hath shall be given, and he shall have abundance: but from him that hath not shall be taken away even that which he hath. And cast ye the unprofitable servant into outer darkness: there shall be weeping and gnashing of teeth."

I go back to the parable in Luke 12 and take what might be a text tonight and speak on "The Stewardship of the Church."

In Luke 12:42 a tremendous question is asked. "Who then is that faithful and wise steward?" Don't think tonight that I am not talking to you. By Scripture I can show you right out of the Bible that God calls every man, every woman, every child of God in this room to be good stewards. "Steward" means "manager." One who has charge of a small store or shop might well be called a steward.

PREACHERS ARE STEWARDS

He uses that reference when He talks about preachers. Paul is writing to the church at Corinth explaining that it doesn't matter so much about what men think of him, so long as God knows him to be right. "Let a man so account of us, as of the ministers of Christ, and stewards of the mysteries of God. Moreover it is required in stewards, that a man be found faithful" (I Cor. 4:1, 2). Thus Paul is designating preachers as stewards of the things of God.

God placed a young man, Titus, to pastor a church on the Isle of Crete. Then Paul wrote him a tremendous letter; it is in our Bible as the Book of Titus. "For a bishop [a preacher] must be blameless, as the steward of God; not selfwilled, not soon angry, not given to wine, no striker, not given to filthy lucre" (1:7). I am saying, every preacher is called in the Bible "a steward of the things of God."

ALL CHRISTIANS ARE STEWARDS

God does not stop there. I am going to show you that God calls every Christian a steward, a manager of certain things. For instance, we read in I Peter 4:10: "As every man hath received the gift. . . ." Everyone in this room has some sort of a gift. What yours is, I do not know. Only God can show you. You ought to be praying, looking to God and asking Him to show you what your gift is. Every Christian has a gift in the service of the Lord.

Now, let us look at the verse: "As every man hath received the gift, even so minister the same one to another, as good stewards of the manifold grace of God.'' ''Every man'' is a steward. When talking about the stewardship of the church, I am not speaking to just a handful of preachers or a handful of church leaders, but to every born-again child of God.

I read of a man one time who searched his soul and prayed until he found his gift. It was the gift of prayer. He found that God had given him a special ability to pray for preachers. He would find out where evangelists were going for a revival meeting, then he would go there before the revival ever started, and get him a room somewhere. No one knew where he was. But he would spend weeks ahead of time in prayer. When the evangelist came and the meeting was in progress, the power of God would come down and thousands would get saved. Finally it was revealed there was a man who felt his gift from God was to keep at the throne of grace, begging God to bless the people, the church and the evangelist.

You too have a gift. Everyone is a steward or manager over three separate things, whatever our gift might be. I am a preacher and have been for 49 years. I was called to preach when I was saved. But God has made me manager over three different things.

1. We Are Stewards Over Time

There is no way to show you how much the Bible speaks of your time and mine. The psalmist said to God one day, ''Remember how short my time is'' (Ps. 89:47).

I knew the Christian principal of a high school, Morris F. Glasscock. He was a small man and weighed 140 pounds. But he was one of the most fearless men I ever knew. He was principal in the Russellville High School, called then Franklin County High School. Morris F. Glasscock in every chapel service every morning in a county high school used to have people quote Psalm 90:12: ''So teach us to number our days, that we may apply our hearts unto wisdom.'' When a preacher was sick or had to be out of town, Morris F. Glasscock filled the pulpit and preached the Word of God. He was a great Christian.

A day is twenty-four hours. A day has 1,440 minutes. A day has 86,400 seconds. The last 24 are gone. You can neither redo nor undo anything in the past 86,400 seconds. God gives us time and makes us managers of our time. Colossians 4:5 is a tremendous verse. Talking about time and how you are to manage it wisely as a Christian, God says, ''Walk in wisdom toward them that are without [unsaved people], redeeming the time.'' ''. . . redeeming the time,'' means seize upon every opportunity or make the most of every opportunity with the unsaved, that is, witness to them, win them, get them saved.

I got to thinking about how the unsaved look at me and you. Do you know that the unsaved judge religion, not from the Bible, not from Jesus, not from preaching, but from Christians? The world tonight judges us, not from the Bible, not from Jesus Christ, not from my preaching or anybody else's preaching; the world tonight forms its opinion of Christianity from Christians. God said, ''. . . redeeming the time . . . walk in wisdom toward them that are without.''

Did you ever think about how much the unsaved understand Christians? An unsaved person understands when a Christian is a good Christian. An unsaved person knows when a Christian is an inconsistent Christian. It is an uncanny thing, a frightening thing, the comprehension the unsaved have about Christian living. They know a good Christian. They know an inconsistent Christian.

I will never forget talking to a man who claimed to be an infidel. I do not know if there really is or not any such thing as an infidel. A lot of people are ''in-for-Hell,'' but whether there is an infidel or not, I do not know. I do not know if there is an honest, sincere doubter that neither believes in God nor in such a thing as a Book of God. This fellow claimed to be an infidel. I was asked to go see him. I went. A lot of times preachers are asked to go see people when those who ask you to go don't think there is any hope, or any use in your going. They sometimes want to see what happens when the unstoppable hits the immovable. So they send preachers everywhere.

They sent me to see this fellow who claimed to be an infidel. At that time on our deacon board was one of the finest men, Freeman Johnson. He was saved one Saturday night in another church in this city where I was holding a revival. A tall, lean man came down to the altar, knelt and was saved. Freeman Johnson became a deacon and was a deacon in this church for some 25 years.

I was talking to that infidel but not getting very far. They want to argue. You can win an argument and lose a soul. Finally I said to him, "You live on the same street as somebody I know very well."

He said, "Who is that?"

I said, "Freeman Johnson lives right down the street from you."

The whole expression changed on that man's face.

I said, "Freeman is no infidel. He believes in God. He believes the Bible."

The strangest look came on that man's face as he said, "I've never known a better man than Freeman Johnson."

Here is a man who claimed to be an infidel, but he knew a good Christian when he saw one. God led me to the subject of Freeman Johnson, and this had more effect on him than any other words I could have possibly said.

God said, "Walk in wisdom toward them that are without, redeeming the time." That man unsaved out there is related to us about using our time. That is what God said, ". . . toward them that are without. . .," in order to reach them. A man out there puts a higher value on Christian living than he does on Christian doctrine. He never thinks much or wonders, *What do those people out there at Emmanuel Baptist believe?* But he thinks an awful lot about, *I wonder how those people at Emmanuel Baptist live.* It is uncanny how unsaved people think of saved people.

The salvation of a man's soul may depend upon what he thinks of you—not so much what he thinks of the Bible, or what he thinks of Jesus, or what he thinks of preaching—but the salvation of many a lost person depends on what he thinks of you, and thinks of me as a Christian.

Now on to something else. Your own estimation of your spiritual self will determine what you do in the matter of time and witnessing to somebody else. I believe that a lot of people never witness or use their time to get somebody saved because of a poor estimation of their own spiritual life. They say, "I'm not worthy. I'm not fit. I'm not ready. I'm not capable. I can't do it," and they do not do it.

God says, "Walk in wisdom toward them that are without, redeeming the time." God has made us managers of time.

Every man ought to have time for his family. Every person should have time for fellowship. If you are too busy for Christian fellowship, you are just too busy. Hear me tonight! You must take time to have fellowship with God.

I do not think I am a good example, but I made up my mind many years ago that I was going to have time for myself so I could read the Bible and pray and let God speak to my heart. I will let no man rob me of that time! God made us a steward over time.

2. We Are Stewards Over Talents

God made us stewards over what the Bible refers to as "talents." Talent in the Bible and talent as we use it are two different things. Talent in the Bible is a coin, a piece of money. Talent as we use it, and as it is spoken of in the Bible, is called a "gift." Every man has a gift of God—I Corinthians 7:7: "But every man hath his proper gift of God, one after this manner, and another after that."

Some Christians draw up like a snail drawing into a shell and say, "Poor little old me. I'm just a worm in the dust. I can't do a thing in the world." You are doubting God. You are contradicting God. God says that you have a gift: "But the manifestation of the Spirit is given to every man to profit withal" (I Cor. 12:7).

Just as sure as I am standing here somebody is going to come up and say, "Preacher, I wish you would tell me what mine is." I do not know what yours is! But I am happy I know what mine is. Find yours! It is there! God gave it to you and He will show it to you if you will let Him! You are stewards of the gift of God.

He has given something to everyone. God is going to judge us for what He has given us. Second Corinthians 5:10 says, "For we must all appear before the judgment seat of Christ; that every one may receive the things done in his body, according to that he hath done, whether it be good or bad." As stewards, we will be judged for what God has given us.

Here is a tragic thing. Did you know you can lose your gift? The parable I read said that when the lord came back, the fellow to whom he gave five talents said, "I've earned five more—ten in all." The fellow to whom he gave two talents said, "I've earned two. Here are the two you gave me and two more—four in all." The one to whom he gave one talent might have said, "Well, I'm not very gifted. There is nothing I can do." The lord asked him, "What did you do with your one talent?" He said, "I wrapped it in a napkin and hid it in the earth." The lord said, "Take it away from him."

I have seen people lose their gift. I have seen men who were called to preach, lose their gift. I could name you a man whom

God called to preach. One day his wife said, "Do you think I'm going to leave my home and the luxuries of life and you give up your job for four years' study for the ministry? No!" He went back on God. He lost his gift! And if you will not use what God has given you, He may take yours away from you!

Take your right arm, bind it to your side for a few days, then unbind it. Now you cannot lift it. Somebody else will have to do it for you. You have a gift; if you are not using it, one of these days God may take your gift away.

I close with this third thing. We are stewards over time. We are stewards over talent, as people use it. I like to call it a "gift," for that is what the Bible calls it. And

3. We Are Stewards Over Treasure

All of these things start with "T": time, talent and treasure. There is no question that, in the stewardship of the church, God teaches we are stewards of material things.

I have a piece of money in my billfold. This one has a picture of Mr. Grant on it. It is a fifty-dollar bill. This is a rare occasion! I want us to think for a minute, then I will ask you a question. How do you feel about money? What emotion do you have? What comes to your mind, what response is there in your mind toward money?

The Bible tells you how to feel. You should feel that money comes from God. In Deuteronomy 8:18 God said to the children of Israel, "But thou shalt remember the Lord thy God: for it is he that giveth thee power to get wealth. . . ." Who helped me get that fifty dollars? God did. Since this Bible is true, what you have, God gave you the power to get. Little or much, God gives the power to get wealth! How do you feel about money?

The second thing I want you to see is, money cannot satisfy. You say, "Preacher, I've heard that so long, it sounds like a parrot repeating itself." Yes, but do you know that there are but few people in this world who really believe that money does not satisfy?

Had I all the money in Michigan, I would be the most miserable man in the world. We can have all of the money in the world, yet be miserable unless we have some things to go with it. We need loved ones. We need Christ. We need fellowship. We need God. All of the money in the world will not make our soul happy!

There are not many people who believe that A lot of Christians do not. They think, "The more money I get, the happier I'll be."

When I was growing up, if you made a hundred dollars a month that was the most staggering thing. We would talk about it, one with another. Mr. Will McDowell worked for the railroad and made a hundred dollars a month. Everybody in the county talked about this. "Do you know that Will McDowell makes a hundred dollars a month?"

You know, you can have money to buy a steak as big as this book, but it will not buy an appetite. If your body is sickly and has no appetite, what good will a steak do? Money will buy you a bed, but will not buy you rest.

How do you feel about money? God said, "Wherefore do ye spend money for that which is not bread? and your labour for that which satisfieth not?" (Isa. 55:2). Money cannot satisfy.

Another thing: you cannot put gold in the place of God. I have known folks who did not have much money but what little they had, they squeezed and pinched it and put it in the place of God. Jesus said, "No man can serve two masters: for either he will hate the one, and love the other; or else he will hold to the one, and despise the other. Ye cannot serve God and mammon" (Matt. 6:24). "Mammon" is a Syriac word for an idol that stood for riches that a lot of people worshiped. Jesus said, "Ye cannot serve God and mammon." Remember that: you cannot put gold in the place of God.

Something else. I don't know if you ever thought of it, but you cannot have your needs by yourself. You say, "Why, Preacher, if I had $100,000, don't you think I'd have my needs?" The Bible says that you could not. Jesus said in the Sermon on the Mount:

"Therefore take no thought, saying, What shall we eat? or, What shall we drink? or, Wherewithal shall we be clothed? (For after all these things do the Gentiles seek:) for your heavenly Father knoweth that ye have need of all these things. But seek ye first the kingdom of God, and his righteousness; and all these things shall be added unto you."—Matt. 6:31-33.

You need more than what you can put your hand on. You cannot take care of all your needs. Oh, you can accumulate; but only God can give you peace. That is why Philippians 4:19 says, "But my God shall supply all your need according to his riches in glory by Christ Jesus."

God has given to the church a plan on how to handle money and be good stewards. Look at Malachi 3:10:

"Bring ye all the tithes into the storehouse, that there may be meat in mine house, and prove me now herewith, saith the Lord of hosts, if I will not open you the windows of heaven, and pour you out a blessing, that there shall not be room enough to receive it."

What a great example Jesus was when it came to giving! "For ye know the grace of our Lord Jesus Christ, that, though he was rich, yet for your sakes he became poor, that ye through his poverty might be rich" (II Cor. 8:9).

God has a systematic plan, recorded for us in I Corinthians 16:2: "Upon the first day of the week let every one of you lay by him in store, as God hath prospered him, that there be no gatherings when I come." What I am talking about sounds paradoxical, that is, that one is to honor God with his substance. Let me illustrate what I mean. We will say, one is to give a tenth of his income, a tithe, to the Lord. It sounds paradoxical. Just suppose you make $300 a week. What would the tithe be on $300 a week? Thirty dollars. Here is a Christian who makes $300 a week. He wants to give at least his tithe to the Lord. (That is kindergarten giving— tithing is.) He has $300. He gives $30 to God. Does he have more here, or more here? I am talking about a child of God honoring the Lord. Is $300 with no tithe taken out, more than $270? You say, "You know $300 is more than $270." No, it is not. You have not studied math. $270 is a lot more with the tithe in the hands of God. Let me prove it.

In John 6 there were 5,000 hungry men, besides women and children. The disciples said, "All we have is the lunch of a little boy, five little biscuits and two dry fishes." But Jesus fed the multitude, maybe 15,000, maybe 18,000, maybe 20,000 people. With a little lunch He fed them all. Then He said, "Gather up the fragments that remain that nothing be lost." The disciples picked up twelve baskets full.

Let me ask you: Which was the most? What they started with, or what they had left over?

I care not what you make. You can make $25 a week. You can be a young Christian boy or girl and have a paper route and make $10 a week. After you have done what the Bible says and honored God, you will have more than you had before you started.

That $300 we mentioned is tainted money and has a curse on it until God is given a tenth. God made us stewards over our treasure.

It seems like a paradox, but there is a purpose in giving. First, that you might receive a blessing. That is the first thing God made me think about. "In all things having all sufficiency." "All things" is what God wants from you. "Honour the Lord with thy substance, and with the firstfruits of all thine increase: So shall thy barns be filled with plenty, and thy presses shall burst out with new wine" (Prov. 3:9, 10). God said He would make everything run over. "Give, and it shall be given unto you; good measure, pressed down, and shaken together, and running over, shall men give into your bosom. For with the same measure that ye mete withal it shall be measured to you again" (Luke 6:38).

God wants you to be blessed. He wants His work extended. He wants you to give to provoke other Christians. The Bible says, "...and your zeal hath provoked very many" (II Cor. 9:2). He wants you to give that the needs of the saints might be met, and that the child of God may be happy. The Bible says, "...for God loveth a cheerful giver" (II Cor. 9:7).

Chapter X

The Great Church at Jerusalem

This is the eleventh Wednesday night that we have talked about the church. It has blessed my heart in a wonderful way to look at God's Word and see what He says about the church.

There are people who, when you say, "What is the church?" immediately think of a building. They want to tell you where the church meets instead of what the church is. I am of the opinion that there are people who do not know really what the church is. It definitely is not a building.

I am sure there are thousands in America who, if you were to ask them, "What is the church?" would describe to you a denomination. Nowhere in the Bible are denominations mentioned. We are a church, a group of saved, baptized believers, a called-out assembly. We are not a denomination. We call ourselves Baptists because the Bible called a man who believes like we do a Baptist—John the Baptist.

We have felt led of God to spend some time on this. There are two more weeks yet to come, God willing and Jesus tarries, on the subject of the church.

Look at a verse with me. It is a great verse in the Bible—I Corinthians 10:11. I want you to look at one verse, then we will pull away from that verse completely.

I want to talk tonight about one of the model churches, one of the great churches in the New Testament. We have talked about various phases of the church, ordinances and officers and orders to the church on all of these ten Wednesday nights. I will talk tonight about a great model church in the Bible. Look at this verse with me before we go to Acts 2. Paul has been talking in I Corinthians 10 about Israel. He talks about the smitten rock. He talked about God smiting and bringing judgment at times upon the children of Israel. Now look at verse 11, ''Now all these things happened unto them for ensamples. . . .''

If you have a Scofield Bible, you will see that the ensamples could be read ''types.'' ''Now all these things happened unto them for ensamples [for examples]: and they are written for our admonition, upon whom the ends of the world are come.''

Notice what this is saying: ''All these things happened unto them for ensamples [or examples]: and they are written for our admonition. . . .''—the parting of the Red Sea, the smiting of the rock to bring water, the bringing of manna in the wilderness, the great feeding of the people with quails in the wilderness. All these miracles happened unto them for examples and are written down for examples unto us. That is why we say you may be able to pick out some part of the Bible and say, ''That is not directed to me.'' You read scores of times in the Bible, ''And the Lord said unto Israel. . . .'' I am not Israel. The church is not Israel. You may say, ''Well, that is not directed to me.'' You are right. But you have to add something to that: it is written FOR you. Everything in this Bible is written FOR Tom Malone. There are some things in it not addressed to me, mind you. I am not Israel but everything in this Bible is written FOR me.

'Now these things happened unto Israel, the Lord brought them to pass to be examples unto us.' Wouldn't you think that the way God established the church 2,000 years ago and the things that happened, also happened for examples unto us and have been written down for our reading? They are for us tonight.

I. THE CHURCH BEGAN ON
THE DAY OF PENTECOST

With that in mind, look at what I call the first model church. It was at Jerusalem. We are going to read from Acts 2. Next Wednesday night, I hope to talk about another great model church that is altogether different. The setting for this one is Jewish. The setting for the great model church that we will talk about next Wednesday night is Gentile. Let us look at the great church at Jerusalem. Now Acts 2 is, for the most part, a sermon. God gives the record of Pentecost taking place. Then somebody said, "What is this?" Simon Peter, led of God, set out to explain it. Let us break in on Peter's sermon in verse 25. I want to read then right on to the end of Acts 2.

"For David speaketh concerning him [Jesus], *I foresaw the Lord always before my face, for he is on my right hand, that I should not be moved: Therefore did my heart rejoice, and my tongue was glad; moreover also my flesh shall rest in hope: Because thou wilt not leave my soul in hell, neither wilt thou suffer thine Holy One to see corruption. Thou hast made known to me the ways of life; thou shalt make me full of joy with thy countenance. Men and brethren, let me freely speak unto you of the patriarch David, that he is both dead and buried, and his sepulchre is with us unto this day. Therefore being a prophet, and knowing that God had sworn with an oath to him, that of the fruit of his loins, according to the flesh, he would raise up Christ to sit on his throne; He seeing this before spake of the resurrection of Christ, that his soul was not left in hell, neither his flesh did see corruption. This Jesus hath God raised up, whereof we all are witnesses. Therefore being by the right hand of God exalted, and having received of the Father the promise of the Holy Ghost, he hath shed forth this, which ye*

now see and hear. For David is not ascended into the heavens: but he saith himself, The Lord said unto my Lord, Sit thou on my right hand, Until I make thy foes thy footstool. Therefore let all the house of Israel know assuredly, that God hath made that same Jesus, whom ye have crucified, both Lord and Christ. Now when they heard this, they were pricked in their heart, and said unto Peter and to the rest of the apostles, Men and brethren, what shall we do? Then Peter said unto them, Repent and be baptized every one of you in the name of Jesus Christ for...."

"For" is a little Greek word *eis,* which can also be translated "because," and is in Matthew 12. We mentioned this when we talked about baptism.

"Repent, and be baptized every one of you in the name of Jesus Christ for [because of] *the remission of sins* [or for the remission of sins], *and ye shall receive the gift of the Holy Ghost. For the promise is unto you, and to your children, and to all that are afar off, even as many as the Lord our God shall call. And with many other words did he testify and exhort...."*

We do not have the complete sermon that he preached on the day of Pentecost. We do know that he referred some eleven times to Old Testament Scriptures. It says,

"With many other words did he testify and exhort, saying, Save yourselves from this untoward [crooked] *generation. Then they that gladly received his word were baptized: and the same day there were added unto them about three thousand souls. And they continued stedfastly in the apostles' doctrine and fellowship, and in breaking of bread, and in prayers. And fear came upon every soul: and many wonders and signs were done by the apostles. And all that believed were together, and had all things common; And sold their possessions and goods, and parted them to all men, as every man had need. And they continuing daily with one accord*

*in the temple, and breaking bread from house to house, did eat
their meat with gladness and singleness of heart, Praising God,
and having favour with all the people. And the Lord added to the
church daily such as should be saved.''*—Acts 2:25-47.

I read down to verse 47 because it is the first time in the Book
of Acts that the word "church" is used. "And the Lord added
to the church daily such as should be saved." All of us know that
we have an example. The Lord Jesus Christ is, first, our Saviour.
The New Testament sets forth Jesus Christ as our great Example,
the One to whom we are to look. We are to seek to live Christlike.
The Bible says we are to follow in His steps. Christ is the Example for every believer. That is why you ought not have your eyes
on other Christians. Learn what you can from them, but the Lord
is our Example.

It would be absolutely unbelievable that God has not set churches in the Scriptures as model churches, example churches. I think
God says, "This is the way a church ought to be." The first ten
chapters of Acts describe the founding and ministry and outreach
of probably the greatest church that ever existed, the church at
Jerusalem.

Notice that the Bible says that the Lord added to the church daily
such as should be saved. The word "church" is used only three
times in the Gospels. It is used 113 times in the New Testament,
but only three times in Matthew, Mark, Luke and John. I think
it would be safe to say we do not find the church doctrine in the
Gospels, the church as we know it, as it is taught in the New Testament. In Matthew 16 Jesus said, "Upon this rock I WILL build
my church...." This is future. Then Matthew 18 says if a man
have a disagreement, take it before the church. Then if the man
will not hear you, the church is mentioned again: take it before
the church. He uses "church" two times. So you do not find the
church, as we know it, in the Gospels. The word is mentioned
only three times.

I said to you when I started this series that I do not believe the church began *before* Pentecost. In the true New Testament church you have officers, pastors and deacons. There was no such thing until the first ten chapters of the Book of Acts. For the church, we have two ordinances: baptism of believers and the Lord's Supper. The Lord's Supper was not instituted until the night before Jesus was crucified. So you cannot say that you had a church, as we know it, before Pentecost. A lot of wonderful people who know more about it than I do, say, "The Church did not start at Pentecost." But in the first ten chapters of Acts we find the record of a great church, the first real, complete church in the Church Age.

The Church Age started at Pentecost. Here is the first church we read anything about in the Church Age, beginning at Pentecost and ending at the Rapture.

Notice that the Lord did the adding. "And the Lord added to the church daily such as should be saved." I am afraid that human effort is trying to add people to the church. That is not God adding people to the church. When the Lord adds to the church, mark it down: those added will be genuinely saved. And when the Lord adds someone to the church, people will be baptized. Two things were characteristic of the people who believed on the day of Pentecost and in the days that the first ten chapters of the Book of Acts describe. One was continuation. They did not get saved today and not be seen again. The Bible says that they "continued stedfastly." The other was identification. They said, "We want to identify with you believers, now that we're born again. We want to identify with you believers by baptism, by immersion in water." So, two things—continuation and identification—characterize the early Christians.

I already mentioned this church. Read on for a few chapters. They finally had the ordinances and the officers, pastors and deacons. So, the church that I am talking about began on the day of Pentecost. Verse 41: "Then they that gladly received his word were baptized: and the same day there were added unto THEM...." I do not know how many believers there were already, but God said there were 120 in the Upper Room. "...and the same day there were added unto THEM about three thousand souls." So there were at least 3,120 saved people.

When we think of Pentecost and 3,000 souls getting saved, I get so excited! I am absolutely astounded at 3,000 people getting saved and getting baptized in one day. Remember, that is only a handful of all those who ought to have gotten saved. Remember, sixteen nations of foreign-born, Hellenistic Jews have come back to the day of Pentecost, come by the thousands. We are told from history that there were over 400 synagogues in Jerusalem in the days of Jesus. We are talking about thousands of people literally filling the streets of Jerusalem on that day. Three thousand of them got saved. As it has always been, others who were unsaved were there, and many of them did not get saved.

Peter said to these folks, "Save yourselves from this untoward [terrible] generation." Of the thousands present, only 3,000 got saved. Oh, we thank God for them! I wish we could see that, don't you? I don't think folks realize that ten thousand or more heard the Word of God and turned it down, while three thousand were saved on the day of Pentecost.

Those who did get saved were baptized. I think there ought to be only so much pressure put on people to be baptized. A Christian ought to be baptized, but I am afraid we sometimes influence people to get baptized. The Bible teaches that when a person gets saved, genuinely born again, getting baptized is perhaps the first thing that comes to mind. That is what he wants to do, and what he will do. Read the Book of Acts. One person after another got saved, and immediately when they got saved they wanted to get baptized. After the Ethiopian eunuch was saved, when they came to an oasis in the desert, he said, "See, here is water; what doth hinder me to be baptized?" (Acts 8:36). He had just been led to the Lord; now he sees a pool of water and says, "I want to be baptized."

Take the folks in Acts 10. When the house of Cornelius got saved, the subject of baptism came up immediately. That is what happened on the day of Pentecost. I am talking about a great church that began on the day of Pentecost.

II. JAMES (THE SON OF ALPHAEUS)
WAS EVENTUALLY THE PASTOR

From the Book of Acts we can show that there was one man who eventually—maybe not immediately—was considered as the pastor or ruling elder. No doubt there was more than one pastor. This church at Pentecost eventually had a pastor. His name was James, but not the James you may be thinking about—James and John, sons of Zebedee. In the list of the disciples are two Jameses. One was sometimes referred to as James the Less, the son of Alphaeus, not James the son of Zebedee, the brother of John. This is James the Less, the son of Alphaeus, referred to in the Book of Acts three times as being the leader and pastor of this church.

In Acts 12, the other James, the brother of John, was martyred. Peter was put in jail and they had the prayer meeting. Peter was delivered. You know the story. The church was on its knees praying, "Lord, deliver Peter out of jail." Peter was standing out there rapping on the gate. Rhoda saw him and said, "Why, he's out at the gate now." An angel had come along and opened the gate and let Peter out of jail. Their prayers had been answered. But these said to Rhoda, "Peter is in jail." Said she, "No; he's at the gate." Peter has something to say in verse 17. "But he, beckoning unto them with the hand [he was standing out at the gate and looking through the door into the house] to hold their peace, declared unto them how the Lord had brought him out of the prison. And he said, Go shew these things unto James, and to the brethren.'' This was not James, the brother of John. This is James, the son of Alphaeus. "Go shew these things unto James, and to the brethren. And he departed, and went into another place.'' I don't blame him. If I had rattled the gate a while and they wouldn't let me in, I would go somewhere else too. That is what Peter did.

Now look at Acts 15:13. When Gentiles got saved in Acts 10, then came this great issue before the people of God. Gentiles are being saved and they have not observed the ritual of circumcision. Now can they be saved without observing the rituals that Jews had observed? That was the issue. Of course they can. So many went up to Jerusalem. Different ones spoke. In Acts 15:7 you read, "And when there had been much disputing, Peter rose up, and said unto them. . . .'' By the way, this is the last time Peter is mentioned in the Book of Acts. Peter spoke. Look at verse 12: "Then all the multitude kept silence, and gave audience to Barnabas and Paul. . . .'' Now look at verse 13, "And after they had held their peace, JAMES answered, saying, Men and brethren, hearken unto me.'' Now, doesn't that sound like a preacher! "Now you listen to me,'' said James. James is in the position of leadership.

Go over to Acts 21:18. This was when Paul finished his missionary journeys. Against the advice of many people, he went up to Jerusalem knowing he was going to be persecuted. "And the day following Paul went in with us unto James; and all the elders were present.''

So there is little doubt but that this church was pastored by James, the son of Alphaeus. One of the twelve apostles became the ruling elder of the church. The Bible teaches, of course, the plurality of elders wherever needed. There is nothing in the Bible that says the church must have just one preacher. The plurality of elders is set forth. Here James is clearly shown to be the ruling elder, the pastor of this church.

III. A CHURCH OF ONE ACCORD

What kind of church was it? It was in one accord. We read in Acts 2:46, "And they, continuing daily with one accord in the temple...." Five times in the first two or three chapters we read the church was in one accord. In the first chapter before Pentecost, when they were having a prayer meeting in the Upper Room, we read, "These all continued with one accord in prayer..." (1:14). We read in the second chapter, "And when the day of Pentecost was fully come, they were all with one accord in one place" (2:1). They were all with one accord in one place.

I mention this for a purpose. As far as I know, there are no divisions in our church. That frightens me, because the Devil always wants to have disharmony. Mark it: where there is accord in the church of Christ, Satan will seek to disrupt it.

Here is a church in one accord. God can do business with a church in one accord. He can get people saved there. God can have His will and way.

God can keep a church in one accord.

IV. A WITNESSING CHURCH

Here is a church that witnessed. What I am going to say is not going to set so well with some of you. But here was a witnessing church. That was their main business. I read in Acts 4:33: "And with great power gave the apostles witness of the resurrection of the Lord Jesus: and great grace was upon them all." This was a witnessing church. Acts 5:42: "And daily in the temple, and in every house, they ceased not to teach and preach Jesus Christ." Acts 6:15 gives us a picture of a Christian, a man they can look at. His face even radiated Jesus Christ. They saw Jesus on the face of this man.

The greatest need in our church right now is for us to be witnessing. We need board members witnessing for Jesus Christ. Board members are not just to sit on a board; they are to be witnesses. Leaders of the church ought to be down at Fellowship Hall every Thursday night. We will never see what God wants to do with this church until we see that happen! The model church is a witnessing church. I am saying that in love. We have a lot of leaders, but few witnesses.

This witnessing church radiated Jesus, talked about Jesus. No wonder so many got saved.

V. A PERSECUTED CHURCH

It was a persecuted church, persecuted for preaching a risen Jesus. Chapter 4, the first three verses, says their teaching grieved the people. The Sadducees came upon them and said, "There is no such thing as a resurrection." That is what Peter's sermon was about on the day of Pentecost, "This Jesus hath God raised up, whereof we all are witnesses" (2:32). The Sadducees began to question. Acts 4:1-3:

"And as they spake unto the people, the priests, and the captain of the temple, and the Sadducees came upon them, Being grieved that they taught the people, and preached through Jesus the resurrection from the dead. And they laid hands on them, and put them in hold unto the next day: for it was now eventide."

This was a persecuted church.

A church in the will of God, preaching the Bible, will suffer some persecution. If a church is not suffering some kind of persecution, it is not the kind of church God wants it to be. You say, "Preacher, who wants to be persecuted?" Hold on for a minute. I hope after I say this you will bow your head and say, "Lord, help me to be persecuted."

In Acts 5:38 Gamaliel had said, "Refrain from these men, and let them alone: for if this counsel or this work be of men, it will come to nought: But if it be of God, ye cannot overthrow it."

He said, "Leave them alone." They had threatened them, "Do not speak any more in this name." They put them in jail. They had already beaten them. They had gotten the word from Gamaliel to do nothing. They probably said, "There is no telling what these Christians will do next." Verse 40: "And to him [Gamaliel] they agreed: and when they had called the apostles and beaten them...." They said, "We'd better whip them one more time." "...they commanded that they should not speak in the name of Jesus, and let them go. And they departed from the presence of the council, rejoicing that they were counted worthy to suffer shame for his name."

Did you ever see a Christian with a long, sad face? "Bless God! I took my stand for Jesus and I'm being persecuted." Run from him. Persecuted people do not talk that way. Do you know what these people did? They did not say, "They gave us a whipping." They said, "Thank God, we're being persecuted!"

Why would anybody say that? Because they realized they could imitate the example of Jesus Christ. He had been beaten. Paul said in Philippians 3:10, "That I may know him, and the power of his resurrection, and the fellowship of his sufferings."

I feel sorry for you little frightened Christians! You're afraid somebody is going to say something about you because you are a Christian. If no one is persecuting you, if no one ever says anything against you out in this godless, religious world, then you are not the kind of Christian these people were!

I remember one time four of us sitting in a restaurant. Tommy and Joy Paige were just getting into their teens. Some people were sitting at the table right at the back of us. I heard my name mentioned. They were talking about and saying bad things about "Tom Malone." I looked around at them. I did not know a one. They did not know me. I just went on enjoying my porkchops and French fries. What difference did that make?

Listen! These people in Acts 5 were happy. They said, "Jesus was beaten. Now we're being like Jesus. Praise God!" Being persecuted and liking it because they could rejoice in that they were prime examples of Jesus.

And they were happy because this was further proof that they were friends of Jesus. The things that were happening were the things Jesus had said would happen. "Blessed are ye, when men shall revile you, and persecute you, and shall say all manner of evil against you falsely, for my sake. Rejoice, and be exceeding glad: for great is your reward in heaven..." (Matt. 5:11,12). He said, "Rejoice." When He said that in the Sermon on the Mount, those disciples might have looked at one another and said, "Rejoice when you are getting the tar beat out of you! How could that be?" Here in Acts they said, "That is just like Jesus said it would be. So praise the Lord!" They went back rejoicing.

Do you know the one thing that got them persecuted? They showed up that old dead, cold, religious crowd who could not help anybody. They had a man forty years of age sitting at the gate. Nobody had ever taken the cup out of his hand and gotten him on his feet until these Christians came along. If you want to get persecuted, then show up a cold, dead religion.

A man stood up in his church in Pontiac one Wednesday night years ago and said, "I want to say something to the church tonight." His pastor said, "What do you want to say?" He said, "We'd better get busy. Emmanuel Baptist Church (our church) could get everybody in the city of Pontiac. It scares me to death."

I do not think we scare anybody much. You show up that old dead religious crowd; you let an old drunkard get saved whom nobody could help; you let someone out of the gutter become a new man in Christ and live for Christ—the godless crowd that has religion but is not saved is going to hate Emmanuel Baptist Church.

They make fun of our old, yellow buses. They make fun of your tracts. They are going to put you out of the shopping mall! They are going to tell you to shut your mouth! We need to do what Jesus and the Bible tell us to do. They were persecuted for preaching Christ and they made dead religion look bad. They rejoiced because they were a persecuted church.

Do you know another reason why they rejoiced? They were innocent, they had no cause for shame. When you see a fellow with a long face and crying because he is persecuted, he is being punished, not persecuted. He did something mean. He is getting what he deserved. Persecution should make a Christian happy. It did these.

VI. A SPIRIT-FILLED CHURCH

This was a Spirit-filled church. On the day of Pentecost they were all filled with the Spirit of God. Acts 2:1, 4: "And when the day of Pentecost was fully come...they were all filled with the Holy Ghost." And Acts 4:31, "And when they had prayed, the place was shaken where they were assembled together; and they were all filled with the Holy Ghost." When they got ready to elect deacons, the Bible says, "Wherefore, brethren, look ye out among you seven men of honest report, full of the Holy Ghost" (Acts 7:3).

This church said, "We have to have the fullness of the Spirit of God." Second Corinthians 3:17 tells us, "Now the Lord is that Spirit: and where the Spirit of the Lord is, there is liberty."

We badly need His presence, His fullness. "And where the Spirit of the Lord is, there is liberty." There is power and freedom. There is happiness and peace. There is victory. And people get saved.

VII. A PRAYING CHURCH

They prayed in the Upper Room before Pentecost came. When

Peter and John healed a lame man, do you know where they were going? To a prayer meeting. They prayed in Acts 4:31. They prayed when Peter got put in jail. They did not say, "Now, we had better get us a good lawyer, because this is serious. They have already killed James." They just went to prayer.

When old Hezekiah went to prayer about a battle when the Syrian army was formed against him, his prayer was far more powerful than the little handful of men he had. Where did Hezekiah go? He went to the Temple, to the house of God. He got down and prayed at that altar. He prayed, "Now Lord, You fight the Syrian army, not me. I'm here praying that You will take care of it." And God did.

Prayer will solve things nothing in this world will solve! It was a praying church.

It goes without saying that it was a church that preached the Word of God. It was a church on fire. It was a church that cared for the needs of its membership. It was a missionary church that kept reaching out further all the time.

What this New Testament church was, our church here ought to strive to be.

Chapter XI

The Ingredients of a Great Church

Acts 13:1

Notice an expression from Acts 13:1, "...the church that was at Antioch." Out of all the churches in the Bible, I have chosen the Antioch Church as the one with all the ingredients of a great New Testament church.

In the Book of Acts, it is the first completely Gentile church. On the day of Pentecost, the Word of God was preached to Jews only, not to Gentiles. Many foreign-born Jews from Gentile nations had come back to the city of Jerusalem and were there when Pentecost took place, but the first nine chapters of Acts are about the preaching of the Gospel to Jews. This Gospel was almost to the Jews only, until it was preached in the house of Cornelius, in Acts chapter 10.

The headquarters were at Jerusalem. From Jerusalem the Word of God went out. The main figure in the first part of the Book of Acts is Simon Peter, a Jew and a great preacher. He was God's preacher on the day of Pentecost to the Jews only.

There is a great turning point in the Book of Acts about where our text is. In chapter 10, Peter preaches the Gospel to the Gentiles. Then the headquarters change. It is not at Jerusalem now, but at Antioch, in Syria. It has to do, not with Jews, but with Gentiles.

Peter, a Jew, is now no longer the central figure, but another Jew, Saul of Tarsus, who was wonderfully saved and becomes the apostle to the Gentiles. He begins to operate in and out of the great church at Antioch in Syria.

Not only is there a change in leadership, but a change of location and headquarters.

The church at Antioch has all the ingredients of a great church because it is the first great Gentile church.

Second, it is the first time and the first place in the Bible where people were called Christians. In fact, the word "Christian" is found only three times in the New Testament.

In Acts 11:26 we read, "And the disciples were called Christians first in Antioch."

We find it again in the Book of Acts where an unsaved man said, "Almost thou persuadest me to be a Christian" (26:28).

Then we find it in I Peter 4:16 where Peter said, "Yet if any man suffer as a Christian, let him not be ashamed; but let him glorify God on this behalf." We find "saints of God," "people of God," and other terms related to a believer, but the word "Christian" is found only three times in all the Bible.

These three instances show the Christian life to be a changed life, a chosen life, a challenging life.

The word "Christian" means "one belonging to the Lord," or it means "Christ's people." It designates Christ as the owner of that person. So the first time a person was called a Christian in the Bible was in the great church at Antioch.

It is more of a model church than the great church at Jerusalem where Pentecost took place, because in this great church at Antioch a tremendous emphasis is placed on the dispensation of grace. We live in the dispensation of the grace of God, the dispensation in which God is calling out a bride for His Son, the Lord Jesus Christ.

The Antioch Church is farther away from the day of Pentecost than many other churches in the Book of Acts.

People say today, "Well, two thousand years have gone by. No wonder they did a great job in Jerusalem at Pentecost. It just happened that three thousand people got saved and baptized."

But the church at Antioch is quite a ways from Jerusalem and Pentecost, yet the job was done. Thousands of people were saved. Here at Antioch are all the ingredients of a great church.

It was a great church because it had a plurality of elders. That is the model way. If a church grows and God blesses it, then it ought not be ministered to and cared for by only one shepherd. Here are named five teachers who were preachers.

Paul teaches in Timothy such things as ruling elders. God never said, "Here are five preachers; all of you have the same authority." "Let the elders that rule well be counted worthy of double honour, especially they who labour in the word and doctrine" (I Tim. 5:17).

God speaks of ruling elders, but here is one of the first churches with a plurality of elders and a plurality of pastors.

It was a great church because it had a great influence on other churches. People went out from that church where souls were saved and started other churches.

It was not a church with just one special emphasis, but it had all the ingredients of a great church. I want us to see what those ingredients were. What does the Bible say were the ingredients of a great church?

If a woman is going to bake a loaf of bread or cake, certain ingredients go in it. If you leave one out, it messes up the whole thing. If you bake a loaf of bread and don't put a grain of salt in it, it will taste different. If you bake a cake and put no sweetening in it, it will taste peculiar. If you leave one ingredient out, it changes the taste and texture and composition of the whole cake.

That is true of the local church. That is the visible church; the church *at* Antioch. It was not *of* Antioch in the sight of God; it was the church *at* Antioch. We are not of this world, but we are in it. So the expression is: "the church at Antioch."

I find at least eight ingredients that make up a good church. I do not know that there is a church on the face of the earth that has all these ingredients, just like I do not know a Christian that is a perfect Christian. But that ought to be the standard that we reach for.

1. A Preaching Church

Of this church, we read of an emphasis on preaching. In Acts 11:19 is the expression, "preaching the word." Bible churches must preach the Word, not the philosophies of men, not rosewater essays that please the people, not pretty platitudes. Here is a church at Antioch preaching the Word.

I read another expression in Acts 11:20: "Preaching the Lord Jesus." When they met together and one stood to preach, he exalted and preached about the Lord Jesus Christ. He magnified Christ and lifted Him up. Christ was the central theme of all the preaching of the church at Antioch.

There must be preaching to have a great church.

I read again in Acts 14:25: "And when they had preached the word...." This church put the emphasis on preaching the Word of God. That is where the emphasis is in the Bible. I am not saying that because I am a preacher, but because it is the teaching of the Word of God.

The emphasis was on preaching in this great church.

In order to have the ingredients of a Bible church, it must, first, be a preaching church. What did Jesus say? "Go ye into all the world and preach the gospel to every creature" (Mark 16:15). I read in I Corinthians 1:21, "It pleased God by the foolishness of preaching to save them that believe." God puts the emphasis on preaching the Word of God.

Some churches don't want preaching anymore. That, thank God, is not true of Emmanuel Baptist Church. Some churches want some kind of ritual or some long-haired music; the preacher is told, "Don't preach over fifteen minutes, because you cannot keep people's attention any longer."

That is not true. You say, "But an educator said it." I don't care who said it. I have seen children listen to a story for an hour and never move a muscle. People look at the television for two hours or more and never get up to get a drink of water. Don't tell me that the span of attention is only fifteen or twenty minutes long!

"It pleased God by the foolishness of preaching to save them that believe" (I Cor. 1:21). God's Word teaches that preaching is the way to get people saved. I read in the book of Jonah, back in the Old Testament, where the Lord said to Jonah, "Preach unto it the preaching that I bid thee" (3:2). God said to Jonah, "Go preaching."

So Jonah, while still three days from the city, started preaching. I don't know whether anyone heard him or not, but he said, "I am going to get warmed up; then when I get into the city I will be red hot." So three days outside the city Jonah started preaching, preaching the preaching that God told him to preach.

I read where Jesus Himself said, "I must preach the kingdom of God to other cities also, for therefore am I sent" (Luke 4:43). Jesus Christ called Himself a preacher.

It is an honor to be a preacher. I would rather be called a preacher than anything else in the world. I don't especially care whether you call me "Reverend." That term is used only once in the

Bible when it says, "Holy and reverend is his name"; but I do want to be known as a preacher. I am proud for people to call me a preacher.

Don't misunderstand me. A man said one time, "I think I might start in my church having just one song and then I will get up and preach." I said, "You do and soon you will be preaching to a wood pile. Your seats will all be empty."

I am not saying there are not other things. Other things, great things, must go along with preaching.

There ought to be good music. There must be buildings. There should be friendliness. You can have good preaching, but without friendliness people will not come.

Many other things play a great part in a church, but the first ingredient of this Bible church was that it was a preaching church. Men of God in ages past who affected the behavior of their generation were preachers. John Wesley crossed the ocean thirteen times when it was a hazardous thing to do. Up and down the eastern part of this continent he went holding revivals and establishing Methodist churches. For a good many years the Methodist church was a great instrument of evangelism. It was because of preaching like the Bible says preach.

Take the preaching of Whitefield, the preaching of Spurgeon, which turned the tide of England. Take the preaching of men like Bob Jones, Sr., who affected this country. Take the preaching of Billy Sunday or the preaching of a Presbyterian, Edward Beiderwolf. He affected the whole Presbyterian movement and drew them closer to God. As a result, thousands were saved.

If we had more preaching of the Word, more preaching the Lord Jesus Christ, more preaching the truth, we would have less communism, less modernism, less ritualism, less emphasis on intellectualism, and we would have more churches like that church at Antioch.

2. A Soul-Winning Church

Second, the church at Antioch was a soul-winning church. Many things come to my mind that ought to be said about this. Acts 11:21 says, "...and a great number believed, and turned unto the Lord." They got a lot of people saved. Verse 24 says, "...and much people was added unto the Lord."

Sometimes you hear it said, "I don't believe the emphasis should be on numbers and trying to see how many people we can get saved." Of this church the Bible says, "...and a great number believed, and turned unto the Lord." I don't find anything wrong with that. I read again that "...much people was added unto the Lord." I don't find anything wrong with that. That is what God wants. One of the ingredients of a great Bible church has got to be that it is a soul-winning church. The normal thing in a New Testament church is evangelism.

Preachers need to be encouraged that there should be people saved in their church. People need to be taught that it is a normal thing in a New Testament church and a Bible church for people to walk down the aisles to accept Jesus Christ and get their lives changed, their souls saved.

While preaching recently in a meeting, I told how the people of Emmanuel Baptist Church win souls and how people regularly get saved. A man stood up at that meeting and said, "Now don't everyone expect that you have to do that. Don't everyone expect to see people saved and say that you have to have people baptized in your church. God gave some one talent, some two talents, some three, some four, some five. You may be a one-talent man."

First, when God talks about talent, it has nothing to do with ability.

A preacher got up and cooled off a group of preachers. Many preachers are just waiting to hear someone say, "You don't have to get people saved"; so they teach the saints, preach on prophecy, or on sex education, devoting their whole time to that and never getting anyone saved. Listen! That is not a Bible church. Even if this did have to do with talent, a one-talent man can preach the Word of God and see people saved. So talent has nothing to do with winning souls.

The normal thing in a New Testament church was to see people saved and baptized. There has never been a day in the history of America when there have been more soul-winning churches than there are today, and yet, comparatively speaking and percentage wise, there still are such a very few.

Some churches are not bothered when no one is saved. Oh, the awful fear I have in my heart that maybe it will stop in the Emmanuel Baptist Church! Maybe people won't continue to be saved. I have that awful fear; but it never bothers some that from one revival meeting, so called, to another, not one soul is ever saved.

Some churches are fundamental, orthodox and still believe the Bible. Once a year they have an annual revival. A few people get saved. But in between, no one gets saved and it doesn't seem to bother them when no one is saved between revival meetings.

It doesn't seem to bother many, when annual reports are given, that no one has been saved in a year's time. Did you know that, in some great groups of Baptist churches in North America, the average is about six or seven additions a year? Whether they get saved or not, I do not know, but that many people join the church, whether by letter or otherwise.

One of the ingredients of a great church is that it should be a soul-winning church.

I read recently of a thirty-five-year-old man who was killed. I do not know whether he went to Heaven or not. God only knows that. I do know one thing. Years ago someone in the Emmanuel Baptist Church led him to make a profession in Christ. He came down the aisle, stood at the altar and publicly confessed Christ as his personal Saviour.

When I read of his death and his going out to meet God, I said, "He is in the hands of the Lord. God only knows whether or not he was saved, but I know there was a time when someone from this church went to him, loved him, talked to him, and he went through the act at least of being won to Jesus Christ. He stood at these altars and publicly confessed Jesus Christ as his personal Saviour."

God wants a soul-winning church. There are people in some churches who could not care less whether people get saved or not. Thank God, we have some who think about it, talk about it, pray about it and work at it. That is why people are saved here.

God teaches that the ingredient of a great church is, first of all, a preaching church; second, it is a soul-winning church.

3. A Teaching Church

They taught the Word of God and nothing else. Acts 11:26 says, "A whole year they [Barnabas and Paul] assembled themselves with the church and taught much people."

When Barnabas went down and saw these people getting saved, he was so thrilled.

Some preachers in some churches say, "Well, if they don't get saved in our church and our denomination, who cares?" Barnabas said, "Oh, I am so glad they are getting saved. I am going to get Paul." So Barnabas searches for Paul. I couldn't help but think how long it took to find him. He had no means of transportation, no means of communication, but he said, "These people are getting saved and baptized in great numbers; now they need to be taught the Word of God." Barnabas finds Paul and "a whole year they assembled themselves with the church and taught much people."

I read two articles in the newspaper against this Book—the Bible. One of them was a take-off on the Southern Baptist Convention. I don't agree with the Southern Baptist Convention. It has gone modern in its schools and in some of the churches. This article said, "We are going to teach sex education in our Sunday school and use the Bible as a curriculum."

In this article, the fellow showed a scene of a Sunday school teacher teaching the class. The caption said, "First, we will teach that Abraham traded off his wife. Second, we will teach about Lot being the father of children by his two daughters."

His take-off on the subject was, if the Bible tells about it, then the Bible advocates it.

The Bible tells about the depravity of man, but God does not advocate it. Anyone who has one eye and half sense would know that. I resent some idiot, who had just a course in journalism, making a take-off on the Word of God. It came out in our local paper, and was in other papers over this country. People responsible for that ought to be ashamed.

No wonder today we have hippies by the thousands on our college campuses. No wonder that we have a city less than twenty-five miles from here that is known around the word as a crime center. We have so many people poking fun at the Bible. But it is the Book of God. It is the answer to man's needs.

Listen! I want us to teach it, teach it, teach it, as we have never taught it before. Sunday school teacher, teach the Bible. Men and women of this church, teach the Bible. That was one of the ingredients of the early church. It was a teaching church.

I don't profess to be a scholar. I do profess that more than sixty times I have gone through every word of this Bible. I do profess to know when someone is lying about it.

This Bible needs to be taught. That is the greatest need. When one idiotic woman influenced our Supreme Court that the Bible should not be read in the schools anymore, I lost respect for every one of them.

When our country turns its back on the Book of God, mark it down: the judgment and wrath of God will come.

I read in Acts 13:1, "And there were in the church that was at Antioch certain prophets and teachers...." Five of them are named. Five in the Bible is the number of grace. So there were five great Bible teachers in this one church who concentrated on what the Bible says in teaching the people. We need to do that.

I was saved and in the ministry and still didn't know one thing about baptism. I read the New Testament through just before I was saved. The young people in a small country church I went to were having a contest, giving so many points for reading the Bible. So in three days I read the New Testament through. The first week after I was saved, I read every word of it again. When I got through reading it, I began to wonder: Where in the Bible did I remember anything about sprinkling someone? Where did I read in the Bible about an infant being baptized before he was old enough to know what he was doing? I didn't find anything in the Bible on that. I kept studying the Bible. I was saved in a Methodist church, but when I went to Cleveland, Tennessee, shortly after that, I looked up a Baptist preacher. I said to him, "I want to be baptized by immersion."

So just at the break of day on a frosty autumn morning we waded out into the water, lifted our hearts to God and prayed. I was baptized and have never doubted since that I was baptized the way the Bible taught.

How are people going to know how they ought to be baptized unless it is taught in the Bible? How are people going to know that they are to tithe their income unless it is taught in the Bible? How are people going to know that they are saved by grace, apart from works, unless the Bible is taught?

The Antioch Church was a Bible-teaching church.

Acts 20:28 says, "...feed the church of God, which he hath

purchased with his own blood." "Feed the church of God." Listen, that is what I like and need. I often say to my family, "I want to go somewhere and listen to someone preach."

I heard a fellow preach not long ago. He, like myself, was a country preacher. He didn't even have the advantage of going to school, but he got into the Bible and got to preaching and I got blessed! I love to hear the Word preached. The Bible says, "...feed the church of God, which he hath purchased with his own blood."

I learned something on the farm. Someone could come along and say, "How many hogs do you have?"

"Fifteen or twenty."

"I would like to see them."

You would take an empty bucket, hit it a time or two on the hog trough and say, "Sooey, sooey," and they would come. They would look in the trough, then look at you and look at one another and say to one another, "We have been lied to. There is not a thing in that trough."

But the one wanting to see your hogs would then see them all.

Take an empty bucket, go out and holler, "Sooey, sooey," four or five times; but about the sixth time you go out and call them and not one will show up.

But watch old Grandma scrape the dishes off into a big bucket, and when she is through washing them, pour dishwater in the pan—there wasn't much soap left in it—then throw the old corn cobs in there and a big piece of corn bread and three or four biscuits left over from the day and a piece of fat back! If you have anything else left, throw it in there, then go out to the hog trough, kick it a couple of times and say, "Sooey, sooey." Here they come. They look at you and say, "You didn't lie to me this time. Boy! isn't this wonderful!" They will get their nose down in it, spill half of it and get some all over them, but they will go away full and as happy as a hog can be.

Many people today are not getting anything. They are not being fed. Preachers are saying, "Come and get it," but there is nothing to get. We need to teach the Bible.

A few days ago my mother-in-law got a letter from a lady friend who had met a young woman who mentioned our name. That same young woman, hundreds and hundreds of miles from here, said, "I was saved and taught the Bible in the Emmanuel Baptist Church."

That is God's way. We are to teach the Bible.

4. A Giving Church

The Antioch Church was a giving church. The Bible says in Acts 11:29, "Then the disciples, every man, according to his ability determined to send relief unto the brethren which dwelt in Judaea." Hearing of a great famine and dearth in the land, "the disciples...." Who was supposed to give? The disciples here are used to represent everyone who believes, not just leaders and preachers. It says, "Then the disciples, every man...." If you are a Christian, God blessed you with an income. And the Bible teaches that it is your glorious, wonderful privilege to be able to tithe a tenth of it unto God. God blesses people for it. You don't lose anything; you gain by giving.

Can we trust Jesus? Can we believe Jesus when He said, "It is more blessed to give than to receive"?

You say, "Well, I'm not going to give." You can't take Jesus at His word, is what you mean. He said in Luke 6:38, "Give, and it shall be given unto you."

You say, "I'm not giving a tenth of my income to that church." Don't give it to the church; give it to Jesus in the church.

You say, "I am not going to give it to that preacher." I will never ask you for a dime. Give it to Jesus for His work in His church.

I will never forget a sweet old lady who was in our church. I preached on tithing one Sunday and she was present. She was hard of hearing and didn't realize how loud she was talking. Every now and then she would say something in the service and we could hear her all over the church. Everyone loved her in our church.

When I preached on tithing, she came forward after the service one Sunday. She lived on a little widow's mite, on a little government check she got every month. She came down front, stood next to me with a little worn-out coat on. She looked up at me with tears in her eyes and said, "Did that mean me, too?"

I said, "Yes, Ma'am, that meant you, too."

(The old Devil said, "Why, you mean man, you! You told that poor woman she is to give a tithe of her income." I told the Devil, "I told her something that would help her more than anything else in the world.")

She said, "You mean I am supposed to give a tenth of my income, my widow's mite?"

I said, "Yes, Ma'am."

My heart was so moved and I said something to God I hope was not impudent: "Lord, if You don't take care of her, I will."

But God did and God always will. He has never yet let one down.

The ingredient of a great church is always a giving church.

Notice that it says, "Then the disciples, every man, according to his ability...."

You say, "I just don't have much." Then the Lord doesn't expect you to give as much. "...every man, according to his ability." Here we have who, how many and how much.

Then notice: "...determined to ...." You have to make up your own mind to do it, then the Lord will put you to a test. He will let all the bills come through at once. I have had that experience.

I will never forget a preacher telling me this: "I had to have

$400. I was putting out a little paper and got behind on my printing bills. The company was about to cut the paper off. I needed money. 'How much money do we have?' I asked my wife. We raked up all the money we had, and that was forty dollars. I said, 'That is the tithe on $400. Take that forty and give it to the Lord in our church.' '' They turned over to the treasurer of the church every dime they had. They tithed on what money was needed before they even got it.

You will find a God in the Bible who likes that sort of thing.

He said it wasn't long before someone came knocking at his door. "Hey, Preacher, could you use a little of the Lord's money?"

"Yes, sir."

"I have $400 here. I am ashamed of myself. I have been putting it in a fruit jar and saving it up. I ought to have given it every week, like the Bible says. I apologize. A little while ago the Lord said that I ought to bring that $400 over to you."

The preacher said, "I thank you and I forgive you for not putting it in every week; but don't let it happen again!"

In I Corinthians 16 we read, "Upon the first day of the week let every one of you lay by him in store...." The Bible teaches giving to God.

Some tithe. Some give a tithe and an offering. I have known some to give all they have. Some don't do any of these things.

The church at Antioch was a giving church.

Why wouldn't one want to give to God who gave all? "For God so loved the world, that he gave his only begotten Son, that whosoever believeth in him should not perish, but have everlasting life" (John 3:16).

God loves you. God gave to you. God wants to give you a life eternal, a home in Heaven, forgiveness of sins and peace of heart.

5. A Missionary Church

Next, the church at Antioch was a missionary church. You

remember that when Jesus was about to leave this world He said, "But ye shall receive power, after that the Holy Ghost is come upon you; and ye shall be witnesses unto me both in Jerusalem, and in all Judaea, and in Samaria, and unto the uttermost part of the earth" (Acts 1:8).

Jesus said in this verse that we should be witnesses at home and abroad. 'Ye shall be witnesses unto Me starting in Jerusalem and witnesses unto Me unto the uttermost parts of the earth.'

So a New Testament church must be a missionary church.

Notice how this church at Antioch was a missionary church. "As they ministered to the Lord and fasted, the Holy Ghost said...." (Acts 13:2). This church is waiting upon God. This church is close enough to God that He can talk to them and the Holy Ghost can say what they were to do. So many churches are so finely organized—so many committees, so many boards, so much program—that the Holy Ghost never gets to say anything. The Holy Ghost could talk to this church. The Holy Ghost said, "Separate me Barnabas and Saul for the work whereunto I have called them. And when they had fasted and prayed, they sent them away."

This church at Antioch is a missionary church sending people out to other nations, to other cities, to other regions, to other territories, to other people. A church starts at home. You start in Jerusalem. But if you stop in Jerusalem, you are not a New Testament church in practice. A New Testament church always, without exception, is a missionary church.

Notice what kind of missionary work it was. Many people talk about missions, and there is a lot going on under the name of missions that we cannot find the precedent for in the Bible.

First, this missionary work was a work of the Spirit. These people did not go to some foreign land for adventure. They didn't go, then find out they were not called. The Holy Spirit sent these two on this missionary journey.

Second, it was the result of prayer.

Third, these missionaries were responsible to a local church, not to some board. Much missionary work is not Bible missionary work. Much of it is institutionalism. There is nothing wrong with institutionalism in its place. There is nothing wrong with schools, nothing wrong with hospitals, nothing wrong with medical centers; but the main job for missionaries is to win people—then the hospitals, then the medical centers, then the schools.

This missionary was responsible to the local church. Many missionaries go out with a church supporting them, but they are not responsible to that church, but to some board. They don't know anything about the church and the church knows nothing about that board. And that church doesn't know what that missionary is doing. You don't find that kind of precedent in the Bible. Missionaries were responsible to a local church. I thank God that many of our missionaries came out of Emmanuel Baptist Church. Some used to be on our board of deacons.

I remember when one couple in our church decided to go to the mission field. He was a certified public accountant with an impediment of speech. Sometimes he couldn't get his words out. He couldn't say what he wanted to say. Other times he would open his mouth to say something and couldn't say it. He was not able to communicate.

One day they came out of the choir and stood at the front of this church. They shook and trembled with emotion. But the power of God was upon them and the Lord was dealing with them. The Holy Spirit was talking to them. He said, "God has called me to the mission field."

Some sixteen years they have been in Ethiopia. He has never yet had an impediment of speech in his ministry there. He is as fine a speaker as I know anywhere. God called him. He was called as a result of the work of the Spirit and of prayer. He is responsi-

ble to a local church and came out of a local church. He has aver-
aged one person being saved for every day he has been on the
mission field for the last sixteen years.

I think of another of our missionaries down in Santa Domingo.
During the first missionary conference this church held years ago,
the Holy Spirit spoke to their hearts and said, ''I want you on the
mission field.'' They answered the call and went out of this church.

I think of another couple. They were capable, intelligent, consecrated, dedicated, wonderful people, but they had not had the
teaching of the ministry of the local church. They came to this
church and were called to go to the mission field in the country
of Lebanon.

I think of three boys who used to be in this church. All three
went into the work of the Lord. They began in this church as small
children, and out of this church God called them.

I think of young people who come to Midwestern Baptist College. They had no intentions whatsoever of being a missionary.
But God said, ''That is what I want.''

Some of our graduates are in Hong Kong; one in Liberia; one
in Costa Rica; one in South America, etc. Listen! One ingredient
for a New Testament church is to have a missionary zeal, whereby
one is interested in a people of a different color, a different
background, a different nationality.

In this church the Holy Spirit said, ''I want these two men.''
They got in a boat and sailed across the sea, leaving the home
church at Antioch and going on the first missionary journey.

So the fifth ingredient of a New Testament church is that it be
a missionary church.

6. A Praying Church

The sixth ingredient of a New Testament church is that it was
a praying church. I read in Acts 13:2, ''As they ministered to the

Lord, and fasted...." Some people in the church said, "We want to go without eating. We want to wait upon God. We want God to bless our church and this work to an extent that we will do without food. We will wait before the Lord and fast."

Many people have asked me, "Do you believe that fasting is for this day?" Yes, I do, if God lays it on your heart; but remember that Jesus said we are not to fast and get a long face so we can tell others we haven't eaten for two days. Secretly, quietly, do it if God lays it upon your heart. If God is dealing with you about a matter go ahead and do it.

This church was a praying church, a fasting church. Verse 3: "And when they had fasted and prayed...." When did this ever change? Why don't churches pray as they used to pray?

I read in Acts 14:23, "And when they had ordained them elders in every church and had prayed with fasting...." It was a praying church. In order to be a New Testament church, there must be an emphasis on prayer and waiting upon God. People must do it separately and they must do it together.

No wonder many people were saved at this church at Antioch. No wonder many missionaries went out. No wonder God wrought miracles in this church. Every time we read of the church at Antioch, we read that they were fasting and praying, praying and fasting, fasting and praying. God honored and blessed them for that.

A man walked into a church one time and asked for the pastor. When the pastor came out, the man asked, "Where is your power room?" The pastor didn't know the man meant the utility room where the switches, the boiler and the furnace were. There was a prayer room and the pastor thought that was what the man was looking for, so he took the man down the hall of the church, and when he opened the door, they saw a group of people down on their knees praying. He said to the man from the utility company, "Here is our power room." "Oh," said the man, "I wasn't talking about that kind of power room. I wanted the room where the lights and the switchboard and the furnace are.'' The preacher said, ''But this is our power room.''

There must be a power room in the church for it to be effective. There has to be an Upper Room experience by the people. There must be a praying church for God to bless it.

Jesus said in Matthew 6:6, ''But thou, when thou prayest, enter into thy closet, and when thou hast shut thy door, pray to thy Father which is in secret; and thy Father which seeth in secret shall reward thee openly.'' Jesus also said, ''That if two of you shall agree on earth as touching any thing...it shall be done....''

There must be collective praying.

7. A Harmonious Church

In the seventh place, it was a harmonious church. We read of it in three different chapters in the Book of Acts. In the church at Antioch, you never read one time of a ripple, or a difference of opinion. There may have been differences among other people, but in the midst of the church body at Antioch, it was a harmonious church. That couldn't be said about the church at Jerusalem, I mean this first church where Pentecost came and where three thousand were saved and three thousand were baptized and the Lord blessed in such a wonderful way.

One day the people began complaining, ''Your women and children are getting more to eat than ours.'' So they got crosswise one with another and as a result, they said they would pick out seven men of honest report, full of the Holy Ghost and faith, and elect them. The first deacon board was elected because of a difference of opinion in the church at Jerusalem. The church at Jerusalem was not always in harmony, but the church at Antioch was. They worked together to get the work of the Lord done.

If we are to do the job God has called us to do, we must have church harmony. There is no mention of strife in the church at Antioch. And there is mention of strife and difference of opinion in the great church that was located at Jerusalem in the early chapters of Acts.

Psalm 133:1 says, "Behold, how good and how pleasant it is for brethren to dwell together in unity!" Let me just add a word to it. It won't really change it any: "Behold, how good and how pleasant it is for sisters to dwell together in unity!" If the brethren are to get along together, then so should the sisters.

There is nothing the old Devil likes more than to bust up a Baptist church. A great football player, an all-American began laughing while I was in his fellowship. I asked, "What are you laughing about?" He said, "I was thinking about a Baptist church where the Devil started an argument and split it right in half. But it backfired on the Devil."

He said, "It is like when you have a lot of cats at one time, you have more kittens! When Baptists get to fussing, all in the world it means is more Baptists."

I went to Ohio to preach. Going through the town I saw a church on one corner with the sign, "Church of the United Brethren." Then right over there on the other side of the street was another church. Do you know what the name of it was? "Church of the United Brethren." I wondered how a church of the same kind got right across the street from the other.

The will of God is that churches dwell together in harmony.

There is a beautiful story about brethren dwelling together in harmony in Genesis 13:8: "... for we be brethren." When was that spoken? One day when Lot's cattle and Abraham's cattle were multiplying, the herdsmen began to quarrel. They had a difference of opinion. They began to talk among themselves. Finally they came to Abraham and Lot and said, "Because we have so many cattle, we don't seem to get along well together."

Abraham said, "Lot, you look to the hills. If you want to go to the hills, you go that way and I will go to the plains. If you want to go to the plains, you go that way and I will go to the hills."

Lot took two looks. He looked at the hills, rocky and mountainous; he looked to the plains, grassy and well watered. Then Lot said, "Abraham, I am going to move toward Sodom."

But Abraham said, "You pick the place where you want to go, and I will go to the place that is left, for we be brethren."

One who claims to be a Christian should treat other Christians like they are brothers in the Lord.

A New Testament church is a harmonious church.

I loved my roommate very much when I was in school. He was in evangelistic work, and so was I. We would go out, especially in the summer time, and hold revival meetings.

One fall he came back to school and told me this wonderful story. He went to a church and people were saved. God really blessed his ministry.

(He was a good preacher. The Lord had used him in many ways. Back in those days, a preacher preached twice a day. Starting on Monday morning, he would have services every morning and night—fourteen preaching services in one week. That was the kind of meeting that I was saved in.)

My roommate said that he started on Monday morning and preached, but no one seemed to be listening. Then he said that he preached Monday night, Tuesday morning, Tuesday night. He preached Wednesday, Thursday, Friday, twice a day, and Saturday. He said, "Does anyone need to be remembered in prayer?" He said not a soul lifted a hand. No one seemed to be interested. He said, "I got so burdened that I couldn't sleep at night. It troubled me."

He said, "Saturday morning, I was so burdened that I could hardly preach. At the close of the Saturday morning service when there was no victory, no power, and when the heavens seemed like brass, I prayed and waited upon God. Then when the service started Saturday night and I stood up to preach, I couldn't. My heart was so burdened that all I could do was weep. I put my head over the pulpit and sobbed and pleaded for God to bless."

He said, "While my head was bowed, a lady got up, then another lady got up. They met down at the front and put their arms around one another and their heads on one another's shoulders and began to weep. Then the whole church began to sob.

"One lady said, 'I haven't spoken to you in over a year. When you came into church you would go to one side and I to another. It is all my fault.'

"The other lady said, 'No, it is not your fault. It is all my fault.'

"The other lady said, 'No, I am to blame,' and they almost got into another argument about who was to blame!

"There had been no sermon preached, but sinners began to come and fill the front of the church. Many were saved. That church was changed.

"On Sunday scores of people were saved."

Listen! A New Testament church is a harmonious church. Don't ever take it lightly. Don't ever think you can carry hatred in your heart against some child of God without doing injury to your whole church.

Thank God, we don't have much of it here to worry about, if any, but a word to the wise is sufficient. Every once in a while you find some in the church who are always complaining, always talking about something and never satisfied with anything. Nothing ever goes right for them. They are not loyal. Mark that person. If in your church the Word of God is preached and many people are getting saved, stay in and be loyal to it. If you don't like the way the preacher parts his hair, tell him so, kindly, and he may have some things to suggest to you!

This business of getting behind the door and stirring up trouble is of the Devil, my friends.

A New Testament church is a harmonious church.

8. An Independent Church

Last, it was an independent church. How do I know that? This is an important thing. This is where many churches and thousands of Christians have found themselves in deep trouble. How do I know that?

After this great missionary journey and the Lord was blessing the church at Antioch and many people were being saved, the church in Jerusalem, where thousands of people had been saved before, was having some problems. Some Jews came down from Jerusalem to Antioch and said, "We want to tell you people something. All these people who are pretending to get saved, are not saved."

Someone said about our church not long ago, "All these people are not getting saved. A lot of that is emotionalism." Then I hope we have a lot more of it. Weeping because your heart is under conviction; weeping for joy—I hope we have a lot more emotion. Folks can be emotional at a wedding and no one will ever criticize. Or folks can get emotional at a funeral and no one will say, "That is emotionalism!"

Listen! we need more emotionalism in the church. A good "holy grunt" every now and then does folks good. An amen every once in a while wouldn't hurt anyone. We ought to be emotional. We have been saved! We are on our way to Heaven! We are children of God! The King of kings is ours! And you don't get emotional about that?

A fellow asked, "Have you got the second blessing?" I answered, "I haven't worn the first one out yet." I'm enjoying the one I got in 1935 so much, I'm still working on that one.

Jews came down from Jerusalem and said, "Now, these people are not saved. Except you be circumcised [an Old Testament Mosaic ritual], you cannot be saved. Without works and rituality, you cannot be saved" (Acts 15:1).

That church at Antioch was up in arms, not caring if these were of the mother church with headquarters at Jerusalem. "Paul and Barnabas had no small dissension and disputation with them" (Acts 15:2). This was not within the church at Antioch; this was with the long-bearded men who came down from Jerusalem and had heard about all these people getting saved. Just like the old Devil always does, they said, "We have more light and go a little deeper than you go. Unless they observe that Mosaic Law, these people are not saved."

Paul and Barnabas had no small dissension, but finally the church at Antioch said, "I think Paul and Barnabas had better go up to Jerusalem and tell those people the straight of it."

Chapter 15 tells where they went to a council up at Jerusalem and told them that these people were saved by the grace of God, plus nothing, minus nothing. In so many words they told them not to meddle with it anymore. They had no mother church. They had no headquarters.

Everywhere I go I am asked, "Brother Malone, what association do you belong to?"

My answer always is, "Anyone I can get to associate with me in the Lord. That is the one I belong to."

They ask, "Are you a missionary Baptist?"

"Yes, I am."

Some ask, "Are you Southern Baptist?"

I say, "I am southern and I am a Baptist."

They ask, "Are you Conservative Baptist?"

"I sure am. I am a conservative Baptist."

"What book does Emmanuel Baptist Church appear in?"

"None."

"But where is the headquarters?"

"Don't have any headquarters."

"You mean you don't belong to anything?"

"I belong to the same thing that the church at Antioch belonged to."

There was only one tie between New Testament churches, the tie of fellowship. You will never find in the Bible where someone in one state owns a building in another state. Each is a local autonomous church within itself—self-governing, independent, with the only tie the tie of fellowship.

They had no officials elsewhere except in the local church. No such thing taught in the Bible. Show me where there is a headquarters that sends out all the literature and says, "Now, you teach this or you are not of our group." When the headquarters goes rotten, the whole thing gets rotten.

Show me in the Bible where it says, "You do what we say or we will take your property away from you." It is not in the Bible. The Antioch Church was independent. No headquarters, no higher officials, no ties but of fellowship, no central property control—this is a New Testament church.

This New Testament church was a preaching church.

This New Testament church was a soul-winning church.

This New Testament church was a Word-of-God-teaching church.

This New Testament church was a giving church.

This New Testament church was a missionary church.

This New Testament church was a praying church.

This New Testament church was a harmonious church.

This New Testament church was an independent church, that is, the local body of believers constituted an organism—not an organization, but an organism called the body of Christ.

I thank God that I am part of it. I thank God by His grace I have been brought out of darkness into light and added to the body of Christ in the Emmanuel Baptist Church.

Oh, God, give our church all these ingredients that make up a local New Testament church.

Chapter XII

The Wrong Attitude Toward the Church

I Corinthians 11:17-34

In this eleventh chapter of I Corinthians Paul is writing the church about some of the things that are wrong. "Now in this that I declare unto you I praise you not," he said in verse 17. In verses 29, 30 he wrote: "But let a man examine himself, and so let him eat of that bread, and drink of that cup. For he that eateth and drinketh unworthily, eateth and drinketh damnation to himself, not discerning the Lord's body. For this cause many are weak and sickly among you, and many sleep."

Does God make some people sick because they do not live right? Absolutely. The Bible does not say that is always the case. Many good people have been sick who were right with God. The most classic example of that is Job, about whom four things were said that were never said about any other Bible character. We read about these four things in Job 1:8: "And the Lord said unto Satan, Hast thou considered my servant Job, that there is none like him in the earth, a perfect and an upright man, one that feareth God, and escheweth evil?" But if you think God will not put you where you can look in but one direction, up, you had better reconsider, for God will do that to a sinner or a Christian.

"For this cause many are weak and sickly among you, and many sleep." Does God kill people? Yes. That actually happened in the early church. God killed two members and gave us their names—a man and wife—when they lied to the Holy Ghost. One came in and dropped dead, and after a while the other came in and dropped dead.

Jesus in John 15 taught that God will kill a Christian in these words, "Every branch in me [every Christian] that beareth not fruit he taketh away: [He doesn't just lift it up off the ground; He takes it away.] and every branch that beareth fruit, he purgeth it, that it may bring forth more fruit."

God deals with every Christian who does not bear fruit. Some He makes sick; some He makes weak physically. God can fix it so you cannot play golf on Sunday; God can get you to the place you cannot do some things on Sunday that some of you do. Christian, you had better be sitting in judgment on yourself, for the Word says, 'For if we judge [or condemn] ourselves, we shall not be judged.' Point a finger at your own life. 'If we condemn ourselves, we shall not be condemned.' If you never sit in judgment on your own sins and failure and faults, at the Judgment Seat of Christ, God will take the place of the condemner. Every Christian must make up his mind where he wants to be judged and whom he wants to do the judging. When God does the judging, there is no mercy. Talk all you want to about a merciful God, but no verse in the Bible shows any mercy in judgment. Mercy is one thing; judgment is another. God will show mercy on none in the judgment day.

We will take an expression out of verse 22 as our text this morning. Paul is asking questions. "What? have ye not houses to eat and to drink in? or despise ye the church of God, and shame them that have not?"

Our text is this question: "Despise ye the church of God?"

There are little variations in the translations of the Bible. There is only one Bible, but in translating from the Hebrew and Greek there are little variations of ways the same truth and thought can be expressed. "Despise ye the church of God, and mean to show contempt for it?" In other words, "Do you despise the church of God and mean to show contempt for the Word of God?"

This church at Corinth was a wonderful church. All the nine gifts of the Spirit mentioned in the New Testament were manifest in it. In writing to this church, Paul said, "Ye come behind in no gift; waiting for the coming of our Lord Jesus Christ." In some ways it was the most wonderful church Paul ever wrote a letter to; yet he said, "In this that I declare unto you I praise you not." Then he said they were guilty of doing something that Christian people ought not do, in the observance of the Lord's Supper in this particular instance. Instead of coming together and recognizing what these two symbolical elements meant, the fruit of the vine and the broken bread, they would come and make it an orgy, stuffing themselves and desecrating the table of the Lord.

Jesus left two ordinances to the church: I would to God we could realize their importance. When you eat at the Lord's table, you are emphasizing the blood of Jesus; you are emphasizing His body that was nailed to the cross and His side that was pierced by a spear; you are remembering the body of Jesus that was beaten, spit upon and cruelly mistreated. When you sit at the Lord's table, you are on holy ground. You are watching a burning bush; you are on holy, sacred territory, and you had better take it seriously. No wonder Paul said, "He that eateth and drinketh unworthily, eateth and drinketh damnation to himself."

Then the ordinance of water baptism speaks of the death, the bloody crucifixion of the Son of God, His burial in the tomb, and His resurrection out from the grave.

We are to give sacred reverence to these ordinances. Paul wrote to the Corinthians that they had not done so. "...despise ye the church of God, and mean to show contempt for it?'' Paul is talking to Christians when he writes this. He is writing to Corinthian believers.

Notice what the church is, who is in it, who is the head of it, and how it is made up.

We read that it is the church of Jesus. In chapter 16 of Matthew, after Peter had spoken of the deity of Christ, Jesus said:

"Blessed art thou, Simon Barjona: for flesh and blood hath not revealed it unto thee, but my Father which is in heaven. And I say also unto thee, That thou art Peter, and upon this rock I will build my church; and the gates of hell shall not prevail against it."

Jesus called it "my church." That is the church I am talking about. No group can claim to have a corner on the church of Jesus, can claim to be exclusively the church of Jesus just because they leave off music in the church or believe in baptismal regeneration. When Jesus said, "Upon this rock I will build my church," He is saying that the church is made up of every born-again child of God.

In Acts 20:28 Paul said, "Take heed therefore unto yourselves and to all the flock over the which the Holy Ghost hath made you overseers, to feed the church of God, which he hath purchased with his own blood." What a responsibility this puts upon preachers—to "feed the church of God, which he hath purchased with his own blood." Despise ye that church?

Paul said that it is a glorious church. In Ephesians 5:27 we read, "That he might present it to himself a glorious church, not having spot, or wrinkle, or any such thing; but that it should be holy and without blemish." The day is coming when the church will be presented to Jesus without spot or blemish. You will never read, study, or think of any institution other than the home that is more wonderful than the church that Jesus said is "my church."

Notice something else. In Colossians 1:18 and 24 we read these two statements: "And he is the head of the body, the church," and "For his body's sake, which is the church."

Is the church important? Most important. That church that Jesus said is "my church"; that church that Paul said is the church of God purchased with the blood of Jesus; that church that Paul said is a glorious church and is to be presented to God someday without spot or wrinkle; that church that the Apostle Paul said is the body of Christ—every statement that Paul made can be said of this church.

This church is Jesus' church; this church is the church of God; this church is a church purchased by the blood of Christ; this church is a glorious church in that it will be presented someday before God without spot and without blemish; this church is the body of Christ.

There is much talk about an invisible church, about a great world-wide institution, about all who died generations and generations ago. There is such a thing as an invisible church, but God never told you to work in an invisible church, nor to be concerned about an invisible church. God is talking about a local church. God is talking about the church where the Holy Spirit saved your soul and made you a part of it. God is talking about a church you can see, members you can shake hands with, people you can sit beside and talk with. He is talking about the local church, not some ethereal, heavenly, far-off institution—a church you can see, the local church.

Paul said, "Despise ye the church of God, and mean to show contempt for it?" You say, "Oh no, Brother Tom; surely a Christian wouldn't despise the church of God and show contempt for it." I believe some do.

1. By Nonattendance at Its Services

First, a Christian shows contempt for the church of God by nonattendance at its services. You may ask, "Now Brother Tom, do you believe that a Christian ought to go to church all the time?" The greatest habit a Christian can have is going to the house of God at all the regular services. If at your church you do not see anyone saved, if the Word of God is not preached and you are not getting your soul fed and your heart stirred, then look for one where you will find those things. I wouldn't attend a church where my soul wasn't fed, where nobody ever got saved, where the preacher didn't preach the Word of God. Every Christian needs a church with warmth and where souls are being saved. Then you ought to be in it every time the doors are opened.

Hebrews 10:25 says, "Not forsaking the assembling of ourselves together, as the manner of some is; but exhorting one another." A good reason for going to church and not staying home is that God said, "...not forsaking the assembling of ourselves together." God said not to make the Lord's day a holiday. Another reason is that word "another." You need to exhort and encourage me by your presence. "And so much the more, as ye see the day approaching."

There are many good reasons why a Christian ought to make church-going his business.

First, for your own sake. Think of the effect it has on you. If you are that spasmodic, on-and-off, up-and-down, in-and-out, kind of Christian who comes every once in a while, misses ten Sundays, and comes again, you are not a strong Christian; you are not a Christian with a testimony; you are not a soul-winning Christian; you are not a praying Christian. I never knew a good, strong, soul-winning Christian who didn't have a church home.

Second, for the effect it will have upon others. If you could realize the responsibility God has given you as a parent, you would be in God's house.

I was in a home the other night. There were two teenage

daughters and a son twenty-two years of age. I was talking to the parents about coming to church. Do you think they ever had the thought that their teenage daughter might go wrong, might bring shame, disgrace, wreck and ruin upon herself and home and, worst of all, wind up in Hell lost and without God? No, they hadn't thought of it. Church meant nothing to them. "I'm so tired," the woman said. The man said, "I usually work." Listen! You had better forget the Sunday work and get in the house of God for your sake and for the sake of your children and for the sake of sinners.

Do you care if the whole world goes to Hell? Do you care if this city is lost and without God and without hope? Then just go to church when you get good and ready. Go every once in a while, and every sinner who knows you will say, "That man (or woman) does not believe what he claims to believe. That so-called Christian doesn't believe that the Word of God is important and that sinners are lost and without hope."

"Despise ye the church of God, and mean to show contempt for it?"

2. By Lack of Prayer for the Preacher

You can show contempt for the church of God by your lack of prayer for your preacher. God Almighty places preachers where He wants them. Preachers are divinely appointed, not humanly appointed. God calls preachers. You have the preacher God put in this pulpit. I have prayed many an hour, "God, if You didn't put me here, don't let me stay another day." I am the preacher God gave you. If you want a strong church, a soul-winning church, then for God's sake, pray for your preacher and for your church leaders.

A few months ago I had to stop two or three times while preaching to ask for the attention of some young people. We have some fine, consecrated young people in our church, and we have some who ought to be taken home, turned over somebody's knee who would wear the daylights out of them. When I demanded the attention of these young people, a few parents turned up their noses as if I were hardboiled.

Last Sunday morning after the church service a woman came to me with a broken heart. "Our home is on the verge of wreck and ruin. My husband is lost and needs God. He came here four straight Sundays, and one of those Sundays he sat between two young people who were talking to each other. He said, 'If I want to be annoyed, I will go somewhere else other than the house of God.'" She then told me that he hadn't been back since.

Some professing Christian young people will be responsible for a soul who goes to Hell, a broken home, and little children without a father. This is God's house, and if there is any place in the world where people ought to sit up and take notice and pray for the preacher, it is in the house of God.

Dr. George Truett, who was known as the prince of preachers, was preaching once when all of a sudden he seemed to flounder. His thoughts went from him; his lips became dumb. He stood for a moment defeated.

Back in the audience sat a godly little woman who knew how to pray. She bowed her head and prayed at that moment.

After the preacher had gone home, his telephone rang. It was this little woman. "Mr. Truett, I saw you today when you floundered and were having trouble. I threw my heart at the throne of grace and prayed for God to bless my preacher and help you to win souls today. In a moment you began to preach again with the power of God."

Dr. Truett said that he thanked God for those prayers of a little woman that day, which enabled him to continue with God's blessing on the service.

My friends, I am God's preacher. With all of my faults, all of my failures, all of my shortcomings, all of my lack of ability, you are duty bound and divinely ordered to pray for your preacher. Samuel cried, "God forbid that I should sin against the Lord in ceasing to pray for you."

Some people say, "I am not as much interested in my relationship to the church as I am interested in my relationship to God." Are you? This Bible plainly teaches that Jesus is the Head of the church. But Jesus is in Heaven. The church, that is, the visible body of Christ, is on earth. Do you think for a moment you could be right with the Head in Heaven and be wrong with the body on earth? Do you think you could tell Jesus, "I love the Head but don't love the body?" If you love the Head, you will love the body, work in the body, increase the body, pray for the body, and find yourself in the body of Christ where God wants you to serve. The body of Christ is as important in many ways to the Christian as the Head of the church.

3. By an Inconsistent Life

You can show contempt for the church of God by a wrong and inconsistent life. Jesus said to Christians, "Ye are the salt of the earth." What is going to keep this city from going to Hell? Christian people. "But if the salt hath lost its savour [not Saviour, but its ability to eat up germs and to preserve], wherewith shall it [not the salt, but the earth] be salted?" Jesus asked. Jesus didn't have an answer for it. And no Christian has an answer for it. If the salt of the earth loses its strength, its testimony, its power with God, how can anyone be won to Jesus? How is the earth going to be salted?

Jesus said, "Ye are the light of the world." Again He said, "A city set on a hill cannot be hid." Also, 'He that lighteth a candle doth not put it under the bed or under a bushel.' Suppose you were to come to my house tonight and I were to light a candle to give us light but put it under the bed or put a basket over it. We would still be in the dark. And you would question, *What kind of a screwball is he?* Many Christians have put a bushel over their light—some dirty habit, or put it under the bed or hid it with worldliness—until people don't believe in their testimony.

"Despise ye the church of God, and mean to show contempt for it?" You do when you do not live a consistent life.

I read a story about a man who lived in Virginia some years ago. He became a very successful farmer, making lots of money. He decided he and his family would move into town. They moved. He kept making more money and he became wealthy.

One night he was sitting in his elaborate study reading a book when his daughter came in and bent over the chair to kiss him good night.

He asked, "Where are you going?"

"I'm going to a party."

He looked at her and said, "You are not dressed for a party. I thought you were dressed for bed."

"No, Dad, I'm going to a party."

About that time the mother came in. God have mercy on a mother who is more interested in her daughter's social life than in her spiritual life. The mother said, "Now, don't get excited. I know there is a lot of her exposed, but this is the way they are dressing now."

Daddy arose from his chair, closed his book, took off his glasses, laid them down and said, "I don't often swear, but I swear to you by all that is high and holy, if you don't take that garment off and dress like a Christian ought to dress, I'll sell this home and move back to the backwoods where we won't have these temptations."

He proved his point and proved that he meant business. God give us more such Christians! God give us Christians who will live like a Christian, no matter what the styles are.

"Despise ye the church of God, and mean to show contempt for it?" You do when you are inconsistent in your Christian life.

4. By Lack of Scriptural Giving

You can show contempt for the church of God by a lack of scriptural giving. This Bible teaches in Malachi 3:10: "Bring ye all the tithes into the storehouse, that there may be meat in mine house, and prove me now herewith, saith the Lord of hosts, if I will not open you the windows of heaven, and pour you out a blessing, that there shall not be room enough to receive it."

In I Corinthians 16 we read, "Upon the first day of the week let every one of you lay by him in store, as God hath prospered him, that there be no gatherings when I come." "Every one of you"—the preacher, the young people, the widow, the poor, the well-to-do.

Three things you should know about scriptural giving.

1. Tithing works. Jesus said, "Give, and it shall be given unto you . . . the same measure that ye mete withal it shall be measured unto you again." If you want God to deal with you plentifully, if you want Him to supply your needs, if you want God to give you the good things of life, be a tither. If you want to get where you can't pay your bills, if you want to be half-starved, embarrassed and defeated, don't tithe.

Many years ago a man came to Dr. Chapel and said, "My income for the year on the farm was thirty dollars. I'm giving my tithe to God." He gave three dollars. Some years later that man came to Dr. Chapel again and said, "My income this year was eighty-six thousand dollars." You see, tithing works.

You may ask, "Isn't that selfish?" Not if you just claim the promise of Jesus and give. He said, "Give, and it shall be given unto you." Many Christians are defeated in every other phase of their Christian experience because they will not tithe their income, thinking of a thousand excuses not to. "The church will get it"; "the pastor will get it"; "I couldn't pay my bills"; "I just don't see how I could make ends meet." If you keep robbing God and making excuses; if you deal with God with a little scoop, that is the way God will deal with you.

2. Tithing teaches. Tithing teaches your children that God is so important and His church is so wonderful that you, as a Christian, owe Him something.

3. Tithing brings joy to the believers. The happiest people in the world are those who tithe. I have never seen a tither backslide. I have never seen one who tithed his income to God who backslid and got out of God's fellowship and couldn't get back. I have never seen a scriptural tither backslide and lose the blessings of his experience with God.

"Despise ye the church of God, and mean to show contempt for it?"

Years ago a preacher preached along this line. A man and his wife down in Texas had some orchards. They began to tithe their income to God. Later there was a blight that killed fruit all over the land. This couple came to the preacher and said, "We would like to give you a nice barrel of apples."

"Barrel of apples? You didn't raise any apples this year. Nobody did."

"We have the nicest apples this year we have ever raised."

"I don't understand that," the preacher said. "The blight was all over the country. Surely it didn't miss your orchard."

"Yes, it did. You remember preaching to us that God said if you would honor Him with your substance, He would rebuke the devourer for your sake? Well, the blight came to a little valley right around our farm, and all around us the blight destroyed, but none came to our farm. We have more apples than we know what to do with. The price is high because nobody raised any. We are selling them by the barrels, and we want to give you a barrel.''

The Christian tither is a happy Christian. Do you want to go around mad at the world, mad at God, and mad at everybody else? Then just keep cheating God. You will be a miserable dried-up soul if you do not honor God with your substance.

"Despise ye the church of God, and mean to show contempt for it?'' Every Christian does who does not honor God with his tithe.

5. By a Lack of Earnest Soul Winning

Soul winning is God's only way for the church to grow. God reaches people through others.

F. B. Meyer tells of a preacher who was in his study getting prepared to preach. His nephew came into the room, looked over his shoulder and said, "Uncle, what are you going to preach on tomorrow?''

"I'm going to preach on John 18:37, 'To this end was I born, and for this cause came I into the world.' ''

That young man looked down at his uncle and said, "Uncle, I wonder why I came into the world.''

His uncle replied, "Son, I don't know, but I know that if you obey God, He will show you why you came into the world.''

He left his uncle's home and walked down the street. A theater had caught fire and people were trapped inside. He dashed in and out, in and out, in and out until he had brought thirteen people to safety before a falling, burning timber crushed his skull. In a few hours he died, but he had led thirteen people out of disaster and sudden death into absolute and perfect safety.

Before he died, his uncle visited his bed, looked down into his face and heard this young man say, "Uncle, to this end was I born, and for this cause came I into the world—that I might save thirteen people.''

My friend, that is why God put you in this world. If you are born again, you are here to win others to Christ.

"Despise ye the church of God?"—I Cor. 11:22.

Chapter XIII

The Destiny of the Church

Revelation 21:9-27

We started back more than three months ago speaking on Wednesday nights on the subject of the church. In fact, tonight is the thirteeneth message on the subject. We will finish it up tonight.

Tonight we will be talking about the "Destiny of the Church," the future of the church.

I think a good place to read is Revelation 21. Five things are yet to happen to the church. They haven't happened yet but will happen just as sure as that Bible you are looking at is true.

Revelation 21:9-27:

"And there came unto me one of the seven angels which had the seven vials full of the seven last plagues, and talked with me, saying, Come hither, I will shew thee the bride, the Lamb's wife."

We are reading the greatest prophetical Book in the Bible. We are toward the close of that Book. We read here that there came one and talked with John saying, "Come hither, I will shew thee the bride, the Lamb's wife." That is in the future. Now you will see described the home of the bride, the wife of the Lamb of God.

"And he carried me away in the spirit to a great and high mountain, and shewed me that great city, the holy Jerusalem, descend-

ing out of heaven from God, Having the glory of God: and her light was like unto a stone most precious, even like a jasper stone, clear as crystal; And had a wall great and high, and had twelve gates, and at the gates twelve angels, and names written thereon, which are the names of the twelve tribes of the children of Israel: On the east three gates; on the north three gates; on the south three gates; and on the west three gates. And the wall of the city had twelve foundations, and in them the names of the twelve apostles of the Lamb. And he that talked with me had a golden reed to measure the city, and the gates thereof, and the wall thereof. And the city lieth foursquare, and the length is as large as the breadth: and he measured the city with the reed, twelve thousand furlongs. The length and the breadth and the height of it are equal."

The city of God is a cube. It is approximately 1,500 miles in every direction.

"And he measured the wall thereof, an hundred and forty and four cubits, according to the measure of a man, that is, of the angel. And the building of the wall of it was jasper: and the city was pure gold, like unto clear glass. And the foundations of the wall of the city was garnished with all manner of precious stones. The first foundation was jasper; the second, sapphire; the third, a chalcedony; the fourth, an emerald; the fifth, sardonyx; the sixth, sardius; the seventh, chrysolyte; the eighth, beryl; the ninth, a topaz; the tenth, a chrysoprasus; the eleventh, a jacinth; the twelfth, an amethyst. And the twelve gates were twelve pearls; every several gate was of one pearl: and the street of the city was pure gold, as it were transparent glass. And I saw no temple therein; for the Lord God Almighty and the Lamb are the temple of it."

I will not speak of this tonight, but He dwells in us. In Heaven, we will dwell in Him.

"And the city had no need of the sun, neither of the moon, to

shine in it: for the glory of God did lighten it, and the Lamb is the light thereof. And the nations of them which are saved shall walk in the light of it: and the kings of the earth do bring their glory and honour into it. And the gates of it shall not be shut at all by day: for there shall be no night there. And they shall bring the glory and honour of the nations into it. And there shall in no wise enter into it any thing that defileth, neither whatsoever worketh abomination, or maketh a lie: but they which are written in the Lamb's book of life.''

I want to connect two verses tonight as a starting place. One is verse 9 and the other is verse 27. These are the first and last verses that I read, ''. . .Come hither, I will shew thee the bride, the Lamb's wife.'' Then we read that none will be in that city ''but they which are written in the Lamb's book of life.'' We see the Lamb's bride and the Lamb's Book of Life in this Scripture. ''Come hither, I will shew thee the bride, the Lamb's wife'' is in the future; it is a prophetical picture.

Verse 10 plainly declares that this is the picture of the church in Heaven that Jesus showed to John when he was on the Isle of Patmos and God gave him this last great Book in the Bible. No one will be in that church except those whose names are written in the Lamb's Book of Life. We are talking about the pure church. A church of only blood-washed, saved people will be in Heaven.

This is the ending of a beautiful story, so to speak. The story usually starts out with the groom seeking the bride. How beautifully that story ends in the Bible! Here we see the Bridegroom gets the hand of the bride for which He died. They move into their beautiful home made of gold and precious stone where they will spend all eternity. It is a happy ending in the Bible for the child of God.

What is the future of the church? Five things are yet to happen to the church that have not yet happened. These five things put together show the destiny of the church.

This church we have been talking about was founded upon Jesus Christ, evidently beginning on the day of Pentecost and continuing until the Rapture. This church, assailed and hated by Satan, is growing. It is being added to every time a soul is saved. The destiny of this church is described by five things that will happen to this blood-bought church.

1. The Church Will Be Caught Up at the Rapture

First, the church will be caught up at the rapture of the saints, or the second coming of the Lord. The phrase, "Second Coming of the Lord," is really a broad term because the second coming is one tremendous, glorious drama that will take place in two thrilling acts, separated by an intermission of seven years of awful judgment.

The first part of that drama we call the Rapture. The word "rapture" is not found in the Bible, but to be "raptured" is to be "caught up." Elijah was raptured. Jesus was raptured, taken up, caught up into Heaven after He died and arose from the dead.

The second part of the second coming is called the "Revelation" because then the Lord will be revealed and manifested as the glorified Christ.

In between those two comings—His coming FOR the church and coming WITH the church—is a period of seven years called the Great Tribulation. The next thing on God's program for the church is the coming of Jesus Christ. His coming is imminent, meaning it can take place at any moment. You say, "Now, wait a minute, Preacher! Don't you think there are some prophecies in the Bible that have not been fulfilled and have to be fulfilled before the Lord can come?" Not a one. "But what about Matthew 24 where it says, 'And this gospel of the kingdom shall be preached in all the world for a witness unto all nations; and then shall the end come'? There are places where it has never been preached.''

If you will read Matthew 24, you will see that chapter deals with the Tribulation period after the church is caught away. The 144,000 converted Jews shall evangelize the world. Even out of the Tribulation shall come a great multitude, the Bible says, whom no man could number "who washed their robes and made them white in the blood of the Lamb" (Rev. 7:14). What I am saying is, there is no Scripture, not one verse, not one word, which must be fulfilled before the Lord Jesus Christ can come.

The coming of the Lord is imminent. It could take place tonight. One reason why I know the coming of the Lord is imminent is because in the Bible a generation of Christians is described as never dying. Paul, in that great resurrection chapter, in I Corinthians 15:51, 52 said,

"Behold, I shew you a mystery; We shall not all sleep, but we shall all be changed. In a moment, in the twinkling of an eye, at the last trump: for the trumpet shall sound, and the dead shall be raised incorruptible, and we shall be changed."

Notice: ''. . . We shall not all sleep. . . .''

I have known many great saints of God. I knew, loved and fellowshiped many times with Dr. Bob Jones, Sr. He went to be with the Lord in 1968. I had often heard him say, "Tom, I believe the Lord will come in my lifetime. And I sure hope He will.''

I spent hundreds of hours with a great saint of God, Dr. John R. Rice, who went home to be with the Lord the last of December, 1980. Many a time I heard him say, "I believe the Lord will come in my lifetime. And I hope He will.'' They were not date-setters but ones with a hope of the coming of the Lord in their heart in a living way.

I got into the car in Houston, Texas, a few weeks ago going to the church to preach. Dr. J. Harold Smith came out of his room.

(Some of my family were won to the Lord by this great man of God.) He got in the back seat. Two men were in the front. I was sitting there. He reached over, took me by the hand and said, "Brother Tom, I believe the Lord will come in our lifetime." He was then seventy-two years of age.

I am saying that it has been the hope of God's people that the Lord would come and find them alive. That will actually happen to one generation. The Bible says,

"Behold, I shew you a mystery; We shall not all sleep, but we shall all be changed, In a moment, in the twinkling of an eye, at the last trump; for the trumpet shall sound, and the dead shall be raised incorruptible, and we shall be changed. For this corruptible must put on incorruption, and this mortal must put on immortality."—I Cor. 15:51-53.

We will all be changed, but not all are going to die. One of these days a group of God's people, who have said like some of my dear friends, "I believe He's coming in my lifetime," will hear the trumpet sound in the sky and the Lord will come. These can say, "Thank God, He came in my lifetime!"

The next thing on the program for the church is the Rapture, when the Groom Himself will come to receive His bride. When that takes place, no unconverted eye shall look upon Him. No unconverted eye has seen Jesus Christ since they took Him off the bloody cross, bathed His body and put it in a borrowed tomb. If Jesus were to come tonight, not one unsaved person would see Him. You and I would. He would call us up, rapture us up to Himself. It is called a secret rapture because the Groom Himself will come to snatch, to rapture, His bride away.

That is what Jesus promised. You connect something that I am going to mention to what I read tonight. I said, "Here is the Lamb's wife in the beautiful Home where the Bridegroom and the bride will spend all eternity." Jesus spoke of it before He left this world:

"I go and prepare a place for you...." (John 14:3). I just read to you the description of the place Jesus has prepared, the city foursquare that will come down out of the sky and the bride shall be ushered into her new home.

The Groom Himself will come. "And if I go and prepare a place for you, I will come again...." A lot of these rotten modernists—and the world is filled with them—deny the truth of the Word of God, deny the deity of Jesus and the efficacy of the precious blood. Those people say, "Now, you are supposed to spiritualize that. The Lord's not really coming back Himself." That is where they are wrong. Jesus said, "I will come again." In a real body? You had better believe it!

When He went away and the two men from Heaven came down, they said, "...why stand ye gazing up into heaven? this same Jesus, which is taken up from you into heaven, shall so come in like manner as ye have seen him go into heaven" (Acts 1:11). He went up with a real body. He's coming back just like He went away. He went away in a body. He went away in the presence of His own. He went away suddenly. He went away in blessing, with His hands outstretched. He is coming back the same way. That is what I Thessalonians 4:16, 17 teaches us:

"For the Lord himself [no ghost, no spirit, not just mere theory] *shall descend from heaven with a shout, with the voice of the arch-angel, and with the trump of God: and the dead in Christ shall rise first: Then we which are alive and remain* [that group that will not 'sleep'] *shall be caught up together with them in the clouds, to meet the Lord in the air: and so shall we ever be with the Lord."*

Yes, the church will be caught away. It could happen anytime.

It will happen before the Tribulation. We have always taught and preached from the Bible that the church will be caught away before the Great Tribulation. Some preachers, some saints, insist they are going through the Tribulation. A few say they are going half way through it. You are listening to one tonight who does not plan to go through one breath of it! A verse or two in Revelation will show us that the church will not be here during the Tribulation.

When the glorified Christ appeared to John on rocky Patmos, He said in Revelation 1:19: "Write the things which THOU HAST SEEN...." What is that? His appearance to John. "...and the THINGS WHICH ARE...." What is that? That is in chapters 2 and 3, the seven churches. "...and the things WHICH SHALL BE HEREAFTER." Hereafter what? The churches. That is why in Revelation 4:1 we read, "After this I looked, and behold a door was opened in heaven: [the churches] and the first voice which I heard was as it were of a trumpet talking with me; which said, Come up hither, and I will shew thee things which must be hereafter." "Come up hither...." Is that the rapture? Here is a picture of it right here.

Twenty times in the first three chapters we read the word "church" (singular) or "churches" (plural). We see it no more on earth until we come to the end of the Bible, where Revelation 22:17 says, "And the Spirit and the bride say, Come...."

In Revelation 4 you see the church—but we see it in Heaven! Again and again from Revelation 4 through Revelation 19 we do see the church—but never on earth. It always is in Heaven after the beginning of Revelation 4.

The church is not going through the Tribulation. The church will be caught up and the Rapture will take place before the Tribulation sets in.

2. The Church Will Be Examined and Rewarded at the Judgment Seat

The second thing to happen to the church that has not yet happened: the church will be examined and rewarded at the Judgment Seat of Christ. It is only for Christians. It has nothing to do with whether or not you are saved. If you were not saved, you would never be at that judgment but at the White Throne Judgment. This judgment is for Christians, where we will be examined and rewarded. Paul speaks of it in II Corinthians 5:10: "For we must all appear before the judgment seat of Christ; that every one may receive the things done in his body, according to that he hath done, whether it be good or bad."

The church is going to be examined. Motives will be examined. Works will be examined and works not done for the glory of God will be destroyed. All Christian work that is not real will be burned up like chaff, but the Christian will be saved "so as by fire" (I Cor. 3:15). He is going to be examined.

The church is going to be rewarded. "If any man's work abide which he hath built thereupon, he shall receive a reward" (I Cor. 3:14).

So there is to be a Judgment Seat, and that is future, when the church will be examined and rewarded.

3. The Marriage of the Lamb
Will Take Place

The third great thing that will happen to the church which has never happened is that the church will engage in a marriage ceremony. I have already inferred such. The Apostle Paul wrote 14 books. Thirteen bear his name. The fourteenth, Hebrews, bears all of his marks and benediction, but it does not begin with his name.

Those are called the Pauline Epistles. That is where a great body of church truth is found. Paul looked upon himself as a spiritual father. He said to some folks he had won to the Lord, "For though ye have ten thousand instructors in Christ, yet have ye not many fathers: for in Christ Jesus I have begotten you through the gospel," meaning "I was the one who won you to Christ" (I Cor. 4:15). He looked upon himself as a spiritual father.

With that in mind, read II Corinthians 11:2, "For I am jealous over you with godly jealousy: for I have espoused you to one husband [Jesus Christ], that I may present you as a chaste virgin to Christ." Here Paul is predicting a tremendous marriage. He already had the revelation in his mind of the plan of God for the marriage of the Son to the saved.

So the church is going to take part in a great marriage ceremony. Prince Charles and Diana's wedding will look like a kindergarten picnic beside this one! The marriage is briefly described in Revelation 19:7, 8:

"Let us be glad and rejoice, and give honour to him: for the marriage of the Lamb is come, and his wife hath made herself ready. And to her was granted that she should be arrayed in fine linen, clean and white: for the fine linen is the righteousness of saints."

It is called a marriage supper, the marriage of Jesus Christ to the church, when the Bridegroom takes the bride.

4. The Church Will Reign With Christ
on Earth for a Thousand Years

Fourth, there is to be a thousand-year period, the likes of which the world has never seen. It is called the millennium because the word is two Latin words which mean a thousand years, *mille* and *annum*.

It is mentioned six times in the first few verses of Revelation 20. It is referred to scores of times in the Old Testament under the headings of kingdom blessings and the reign of our Lord upon this earth. "Blessed and holy is he that hath part in the first resurrection"—that is you and me. The first resurrection is the Christian resurrection. "...on such the second death hath no power, but they shall be priests of God and of Christ and shall reign with him a thousand years.''

Did you ever stop to think that no man has ever lived on earth a thousand years. One fellow came very close. If he had lived 31 more years, he would have made it. Methuselah was 969. No man has ever lived longer than he. But every Christian is going to live on this renovated earth and reign with Christ a thousand years. It will be a reign of righteousness. Men will lay down their spears and take up their pruning hooks. Men shall live with Christ a thousand years in a reign on earth.

5. He Will Demonstrate His Glory to Us Through All Eternity

Here is something else yet to happen in the destiny of the church. We are going to live with Him throughout all eternity. Ephesians is the "in" book. One time I took a red pencil and marked all the times I found the word "in." I think 23 times in just one chapter I drew a little red ring around the word "in." "In Christ," "in Christ"—one chapter over and over. It shows us "in him, in heavenly places." We read, ". . . he hath made us accepted in the beloved." "And you hath he quickened [made alive] who were dead in trespasses and sins" (2:1). "And hath raised us up together, and made us sit together in heavenly places. . ." (2:6). God sees you tonight seated in the heavenlies. Why?

Here is God's answer, also found in Ephesians, "That in the ages to come he might shew the exceeding riches of his grace in his kindness toward us through Christ Jesus" (2:7). God is going to put you and me on exhibition as demonstrations of the grace of God! We are going to be on parade throughout all eternity. The destiny of the church is that in the ages to come God Himself will show the exceeding riches of His grace and His kindness to you and me through Christ Jesus! What a destiny!

I repeat what I said at the beginning. It is a story with a happy ending, the story of the church that has soaked the earth with the blood of its martyrs. It has a happy ending. For He who died for the bride will one day lead her to the marriage altar and to the beautiful Home for all eternity.

Chapter XIV

The Kind of Church Jesus Is Building

Matthew 16:13-27

That church Jesus is building may not be the church that you have in mind, and it may be different from what you see visibly and physically as you look at the work of God; but the Bible clearly teaches that Jesus is building a certain kind of New Testament Bible church.

Great numbers don't always mean a great church. Don't misunderstand me; I am for numbers. And God is. God wants every man and woman, every boy and girl to hear the Word of God and be saved. I don't agree in any sense with these people who say that God is not for great numbers. That is not true. One who does not believe in numbers would not get very far in the Bible before running into a problem. The fourth book of the Bible is called the Book of Numbers. I am positive it is the will of God that we reach every person we possibly can. I don't agree with those who say our church has gotten so large that we don't know the people and don't have good close fellowship. I disagree with these folks who say you cannot have a spiritual church and a large church at the same time. It is estimated that 30,000 people heard the Word of God and believed and were baptized in 12 months in the city of Jerusalem, in that first church after Pentecost.

But great numbers do not necessarily mean a great church. The word "church" is taken from the Greek word *ekklesia* meaning "called-out ones." And that's the work of God, churches made up of born-again, baptized people who are genuinely saved and have been called out of sin and out of the world. But great numbers do not necessarily mean it is the kind of church Jesus had in mind when He said, "Upon this rock I will build my church."

Great buildings do not necessarily mean a great church. I remind you again that the early church had no buildings. These Christians who turned the world upside down, these people who saw folks saved and baptized by the thousands, owned no church property whatsoever. They had no church buildings, no Sunday school buses, no pews, no P. A. system, no musical instruments. They had no material equipment at all. So great buildings do not necessarily mean a great church, though it is necessary to have them. These are a vital part of reaching people for Christ. But great buildings do not necessarily mean a great church.

In a sense the church is the hope of all mankind. Now I know immediately it will come to your mind, "The Lord is the hope of all mankind." That is certainly true. But I would remind you that the Great Commission or the command to evangelize the world was given to the church of the Lord Jesus Christ. If the church of Jesus does not get people saved, does not send out the Word of God around the world, then the world will never be evangelized. And so in a sense we can say the church is the hope of all mankind. "Go ye into all the world, and preach the gospel to every creature" is the command God has given to the church. But in most cases the church has failed in its program to evangelize the world.

Now Jesus said, "I will build my church. . . ." I would remind you that the foundation of the church is Jesus Christ. I am not primarily concerned today with explaining what this verse means. You see a conversation in this chapter between Jesus and Peter. Jesus asked the question, "Whom do men say that I the Son of man am?" Different groups gave Him various answers. But then Jesus said, "But whom say ye that I am?"

Simon Peter was most always the spokesman for the crowd. He was the impetuous, forward type, an out-going person who usually spoke up before anyone else, sometimes speaking before putting his brain in gear. And what he said was not always wise. In fact, in this chapter, when Jesus said some things about going to the cross and dying for the sins of the world, Peter said, "Be it far from thee, Lord: this shall not be unto thee." Jesus gave the sternest rebuke I think He ever gave to a Christian: "Get thee behind me, Satan," talking to Simon Peter. Peter was no more perfect than I am or you are.

But here Simon Peter answered Jesus' statement, "But whom say ye that I am?" by saying, "Thou art the Christ, the Son of the living God." In other words, "You are the divine Son of God. You are no ordinary man. You are not just a great teacher or a great philosopher. You are God's Son in the flesh. Jesus said, "Blessed art thou, Simon Bar-jona: for flesh and blood hath not revealed it unto thee, but my Father which is in heaven." In other words, "Peter, God made this plain to you." Then He said, "And I say also unto thee, That thou art Peter, and upon this rock I will build my church...."

I don't want to be technical but some folks say that the Lord is saying unto Peter, "I am going to build a church upon you." That's a ridiculous statement. If you study carefully all of this chapter and other verses that throw light on it, you will know He said, "Thou art Peter...." There is a play on words here. "Peter" comes from the word *petros* and the word "rock" comes from the word *petra* and this is what the Lord is saying: "...thou art

Peter.... [the little stone], but upon this rock [the great stone, the rock just brought into focus and prominence by the testimony of Simon Peter that Jesus Christ is the Son of God], I will build my church; and the gates of hell shall not prevail against it.''

Now a Bible, New Testament church must be molded after Bible, New Testament churches. If you were to ask any honest Christian in this house this morning, ''What kind of a Christian do you think a Christian ought to be?'' he would answer, ''A Christian ought to be the kind of Christian that Christians were in Bible times.'' That is true; but it is equally as true that the church ought to be the kind of church Jesus was building in New Testament times.

Now what kind of a church is Jesus talking about? When the day of Pentecost came and this great group of believers were baptized into one great body, the Holy Spirit of God began to work in the building of this church Jesus referred to in this verse. ''...upon this rock I will build my church; and the gates of hell shall not prevail against it.''

1. It Was a Praying Church

First, these were a praying people. Go back to the Book of Acts and read about this church that God was working in, and this church God was working through, and this church God brought together. Study that church and you will find what the first characteristic of that group of believers was.

Before Pentecost ever came, 120 believers were in an Upper Room waiting for the promise of Jesus to be fulfilled, that the Holy Ghost would come. What does the Bible say they were doing? Acts 1:14: ''These all continued with one accord in prayer and supplication....'' The very first characteristic you read about in the church Jesus built was that it was a praying church.

That same characteristic will be found wherever you find a New

Testament church. Wherever you find a New Testament church, you find a group of people who know what it means to get on their knees and pray until God hears them and works miracles for them. It was a praying church.

Read again in Acts 4:31, "And when they had prayed, the place was shaken where they were assembled together. . . ." Always praying in this fourth chapter of the Book of Acts.

These were a persecuted people. When told, "You can't speak anymore in the name of Jesus," they did anyway. And they continued to witness. And they continued to be persecuted. They were imprisoned and beaten. When they came together as a result of persecution, what did they do? They had a prayer meeting. God gave them new boldness. God gave them new grace. They just kept on witnessing for the Lord. This was a praying church.

You read about it again in Acts 12. It looked as if something was about to happen in this church Jesus was building that would just about put them out of business. They arrested Simon Peter and James, two of the great leaders, and took a sword and cut off James' head. They meant business.

But they put Simon Peter in jail. "We will put him in jail and later on execute him." There in that jail is Simon Peter. Yonder in the home of John Mark a group have gathered together. They are praying, "Lord, our preacher is in jail, the one who preached on the day of Pentecost. He is to be executed. We can't tear down those iron bars. We have no authority over these who have arrested him. But we can pray." And pray they did. The church went to God in prayer and supplication.

While the people are praying, God is working. That has always been the case. You may not think it very exciting and very dramatic, but you will never know all the blessing of God until you know what it means to have your prayers answered.

This church was praying. God was working. Simon Peter was

in jail and sleeping. Some of you are saying, "I don't know how that preacher could go to sleep knowing that his friend James has had his head cut off and knowing the same fate was about to be his." But Peter just laid down in that jail and went to sleep. His hands and feet were chained to soldiers. And soldiers were out at the gate. I get a bit amused at this. Those folks kind of suspicioned something unordinary, something unusual might happen. And it did. An angel came that night, shook Simon Peter and said, "Get up and out of here. You are released." Simon Peter got up, the chains fell off, the gates opened, and those soldiers became as helpless as dead men while Simon Peter walked out of that jail in answer to prayer.

Down at Mark's house Christians are praying. There is a little woman there, Rhoda by name. Like a lot of other folks, Rhoda may have gotten tired of praying. Too, the floor is hard and all these older folks are praying these long prayers. So Rhoda began to look around. She heard a rattle at the front gate. Looking out, she sees Simon Peter. She cries out, "Peter is here! Your prayers are answered!"

Some soul said, "Be quiet, Rhoda. You are disturbing the prayer meeting."

"But Peter is at the gate."

"Rhoda, you are having nightmares, hallucinations. You are seeing things you ought not to see. Your mind has blown up on you."

"I tell you, Peter is at the gate."

They look up and sure enough—there he is! For God heard a praying group of people.

The church Jesus built was a praying church.

Someone reminded me the other night of a Saturday night of prayer held in this church some months ago when every hour of the night, all night long, people knelt at these altars invoking God's blessing upon this place, and the next day, Sunday, 156 people who were saved followed the Lord in baptism in one day and united with this church. God's people praying had as much, if not more, to do with that than anything else in the world.

God answers prayer.

Wherever you find individuals in the Book of Acts, you find them praying. Peter and John went up to the Temple at the hour of prayer. Peter, when the Lord spoke to him about the house of Cornelius, had gone up on the roof top to pray. Paul too was a man of prayer.

So the church Jesus built was a praying church.

I read a funny story. An old skeptic didn't believe in the church. Not much happened there, hardly anybody got saved, the crowds were small, so this skeptic didn't much believe in it. He was skeptical about everything.

A deacon was always talking about his religion, and the church and how pious he was. And this deacon was continually condemning this old skeptic. One day the church building caught on fire. Somebody said, "The church house is burning down! We need all the help to get the fire out." It is said the old deacon and skeptic started running side by side, going to put the fire out. The deacon said to the skeptic, "Well, I've never seen you running to get to the church before." The skeptic said, "Well, I've never seen the church on fire before either."

Say what you will, but what this world needs more than anything is to see the church on fire, to see something unusual, something out of the ordinary, to see a work wrought that even unsaved people will have to say, "God is working in that church."

So the church Jesus built was, first of all, a praying church.

2. It Was a Giving Church

I am going to depart from what I believe is the regular order and the regular sequence of things in the Book of Acts and the New Testament.

But the church Jesus built was a giving church. I beg of you this morning, be honest with God. Read the Book of Acts. You read of the day of Pentecost in chapter 2, how 3,000 were saved and baptized, how miracles were wrought and prayers were answered. But you read in verse 45 of Acts chapter 2 that these people sold their possessions and parted them to all, as every man had need. Now I do not believe the Bible teaches that God wants everybody to sell their goods, liquidate all their assets and give it to the Lord. But that is what these early Christians did. Then there is a development of teaching on giving in the rest of the New Testament. But we read, ''...and sold their possessions and goods, and parted them to all men, as every man had need.''

The first man to tithe was Abraham, in Genesis chapter 14. You read twice this expression, ''He gave him tithes of all'' (vs. 20). You read twice this expression, ''...God, possessor of heaven and earth'' (vs. 19). In other words, God owns everything you have: the home in which you live, the clothes that keep you warm, the bread and water you put in your body. He is the ''possessor of heaven and earth.'' Oh, to find a child of God who will recognize that and will enter into a covenant with God to share with Him all he has! God is the possessor of Heaven and earth.

So, these people ''sold their possessions and goods, and parted them to all men, as every man had need.'' You find an individual case mentioned. In Acts 4:37 is a man by the name of Barnabas who ''having land, sold it, and brought the money, and laid it at the apostles' feet.''

Don't just shake your head at this and say, ''The preacher is always talking about money.'' Why do I preach about money? I might give three reasons. First, the Bible teaches it. And I have been told by God to declare the whole counsel of God. And I cannot preach the Bible without preaching on the matter of giving. I preach about giving because I want to see Christian people get the most out of their Christian life. And I feel sorry for that Christian who, either because of selfishness or ignorance of the Word of God, has never known the thrill and joy of giving to the Lord Jesus Christ. I preach about it because without it, the world will go to Hell, and we need to evangelize the world. The Bible mentions that Barnabas sold his land, brought it and said, "Use this to send the Gospel out further and further."

Sometimes people say, "Don't you get embarrassed talking about money?" No! I wish you could see what I see when I do talk about it. I see some of the strangest expressions. While you are singing, or making the announcements, or giving the Devil to the folks on the outside, they are with you 100 percent. They have that radiant countenance and that happy expression like, "Give it to them, Preacher!" But when you get on this, the same ones look as if all of a sudden they have developed a stomachache or something terrible is happening down inside and they are going to die any minute. If you could see what I see when I get on this!

If I were to ask you, "What is most of chapter 5 of Acts about?" I wonder if you would really know. It's about a man named Ananias and his wife Sapphira. They saw Barnabas come and give to the Lord bountifully, heartily and with joy and blessing. No doubt people said, "You know that's wonderful. Barnabas must love God. That magnanimous soul wants the Gospel to be sent out, so he has given all that a man can give."

Ananias and Sapphira, hearing the people talk about it, said, "Let's pretend we have done that." They had a farm and sold it. Now God didn't demand that they sell it. They took part of that money and hid it. But they brought a part of it and said, "We have sold our lands and here is the money. We're giving it all to God." God looked down from Heaven and said, "I will not let a man be a hypocrite in his giving," so He struck Ananias dead.

Along came his wife. Preacher Peter said, "You sold your farm for how much?" She told the same lie as her husband. He said, "The feet of them who just carried your husband out of here are on their way to carry you out." God killed two members of that church because of their hypocrisy in the matter of giving.

You say, "Preacher, that's strong punishment." Yes, and it strikes fear into my heart and makes me know that God means business in the matter of honoring Him.

This church was a giving church. When Jesus said, "I will build my church," He was talking about a praying church and a giving church.

3. It Was a Soul-Winning Church

He was also talking about a soul-winning church. Now Jesus had already taught the Christian's responsibility in getting people saved. One of the first challenges Jesus ever gave was, "Follow me, and I will make you fishers of men." And when Jesus said, "...upon this rock I will build my church...," He was talking about a soul-winning church.

A church where people do not get saved is not a New Testament, Bible-believing church. A church where lives are not changed is not a church that Jesus built. It is a society, it is a gathering of people, but not a New Testament church like Jesus built. Acts 2:41 says, "Then they that gladly received his word were baptized: and the same day there were added unto them about three thousand souls." The most outstanding event about this church Jesus was building in the Book of Acts was that people got saved in that church. Acts 4:4, "Howbeit many of them which heard the word believed; and the number of the men was about five thousand." Five thousand men were saved, to say nothing of women and children, shortly after the day of Pentecost.

Oh, if God would take these eighteen words of Acts 5:42 and grip my heart and yours, how thankful I would be to Him! "And daily in the temple, and in every house, they ceased not to teach and preach Jesus Christ."

The church Jesus built was a soul-winning church, not just a teaching church. Some folks say, "I like to go to a church where the preacher takes the Bible and teaches the Word of God and doesn't step on our toes and doesn't talk about other people's religion." That would be more comfortable, I guess. But the church Jesus built was not just a teaching church, not just where a group of folks got together and gave to missions.

When this church first started folks would give me a card and say, "I want you to call on So-and-so." I had a pocketful of them. Every time I saw some of our people I would get more of them. I was the depository for all the calling cards.

One day I got the idea they were saying, "Let Brother Tom do the calling. We will just supply him with the contacts." So I got me some cards and put down the names of people I knew who needed to be called on. Then when somebody came along and said, "Brother Tom, I want you to call on this person," I would say, "I'd be glad to," and reach in my pocket and get out a card and say, "And I would like for you to call on this one." We have been playing cards in our church for thirty years, and I hope the Lord will help us to keep playing cards!

But one day a man handed me a little piece of thin cardboard about the size of that piece of paper. He was an oil truck driver and that little piece of cardboard had smudges of oil or grease on it and it had a lady's name and address. This man in our church said, "Would you call on this person? She needs to be saved." So a day or two later I put that piece of dirty cardboard in my pocket and drove to the northwest side of the city and found that address. I knocked on the door. An old lady came to the door. I didn't know she was seventy-nine until she told me later. She asked me to come in. I told her that all had sinned and come short of the glory of God. I told her that Jesus came and, for my sin and hers, took our place on the cross. The big tears began to roll down her cheeks. She said, ''Well, I need to be saved. I have been so lonely. When I was fifty years old my husband died. We raised five children, all grown and married and gone. I have been practically alone for twenty-nine years.''

I said, ''You don't have to be alone any longer. Someone will come into your heart, into your home and be with you all the rest of your days.''

''That's what I want,'' she said. She was still sitting on the couch, and I stood in front of her with a little New Testament. I read her the story of Jesus and said, ''Would you like to be saved?''

''Oh, yes, Preacher, I would love to be saved. I want Christ in my life.''

I asked her if she would get down on her knees, and that sweet soul got down on her knees. I got down beside her and prayed. She wept and God saved her.

There is no greater joy than that! I walked out on the porch and all of a sudden something dawned on me. Across the street from the little home where a woman had lived many years, twenty-nine years all alone, was a church whose pastor always talked about the deeper life, foreign missions, the fullness of the Holy Spirit—all of which are great.

I turned around and knocked on the door again and this old lady came to the door. She had her handkerchief and was drying her tears. ''Did you forget something, Mr. Malone?''

I said, ''I want to ask you a question if you don't mind. You have lived here these many years and twenty-nine years you have been all alone.''

She said, ''That's right.'' And she started talking about it again.

"My children are married and they have responsibilities and I rarely ever see any of them. I have been just practically alone for twenty-nine years."

I said, "Lady, has anyone ever knocked on your door and told you how to be saved? Has anybody ever asked you if you were a Christian?" (She had told me she had lived in the Pontiac area all her life.)

She thought for a minute and said, "No! They never have. Now maybe one person came awfully close to it. A man who drives an oil truck brought fuel oil to my home a few days ago and said to me, 'Lady, I am going to ask my preacher, Brother Malone, to come and see you.' " (That's the man who gave me the little piece of greasy cardboard.)

I said, "Thank you, Ma'am. I will be praying for you and be back to see you," and stepped out on the porch.

My heart was broken. I thought, *There is a church across the street. For twenty-nine years no Christian ever knocked on the door of a lost person.* And I thought of how close that dear soul was to Hell. Then I asked God, like I have asked Him a thousand times, "O God, forgive me for not being a better soul winner."

Listen, friend! The church Jesus built was a soul-winning church and that's the kind God wants this church to be.

"...upon this rock I will build my church...."

4. It Was a Loving Church

The church that Jesus built was also a loving church. That church was literally baptized and filled with a God-given love shed abroad in the hearts of these people by the Holy Spirit. It was a loving church.

Acts, chapter 6, is the record of the election of the first deacon board that we know anything about. Now the word "deacon" is not found in that chapter, but it is found five times in the New

Testament—in I Timothy, chapter 3; in the first verse or two of the Philippians letter. But it is not found in chapter 6 of the Book of Acts. It arose because there was a problem, growing pains if you please, in the church. There were two different kinds of Jews: those Jews who were natives of the land of Palestine and those Jews who came to observe the great religious feast, and when Pentecost took place, etc. They were Hellenistic Jews and there were Palestinian Jews. One day the Hellenistic Jews, that is, the ones who came from afar, came to the apostles and said, ''Now when folks are being fed and the needs of widows and children and people in this church are taken care of, we are not getting our share of this.'' And there was a murmuring and complaining. And the apostles said, ''Wherefore, brethren, look ye out among you seven men of honest report, full of the Holy Ghost and wisdom, whom we may appoint over this business'' (Acts 6:3). They said, ''It is not wise that we leave the Word of God to serve tables, and we will elect a deacon board for that purpose.''

And from that day till this I have heard all kinds of remarks and all kinds of criticisms about deacons in Baptist churches. Many times jokes are made about deacons. Many times criticisms are made about deacons. There has probably been as much hatred about deacons and their activity and the relationship of other people to them, as anything else mentioned in the New Testament church.

But I have never seen a greater demonstration of love than in the election of those seven deacons. These apostles said to these foreign-born Jews, ''You pick out seven men.'' Here were two factions. Every one of them was from the faction that seemed to be getting the least out of the daily ministration. In other words, one group said, ''We love these people. We do not want them deprived. Elect a whole deacon board out of that crowd.'' I do not find in all of the Bible a greater demonstration of Christian love than I do in the election of the first deacon board. That spirit permeated the whole New Testament church, the church that Jesus built.

You hear about it but we are selfish, self-centered. You hear preachers preach about how a Christian ought to have the love of God shed abroad in his heart by the Holy Ghost, but when you get ready to hate somebody, you're going to hate him, no matter what. And that's the way many Christians live. But that is not Bible Christianity. Bible Christians were absorbed, literally bathed, in a divine love. We see the manifestation of that love even in the election of the first deacon board.

I do not know of any stronger language found in the Bible than that of a Christian and Christian love. First John 2:10, 11 says, "He that loveth his brother abideth in the light, and there is none occasion of stumbling in him." I say Christians have backslid and stumbled, have lost their joy and the power of God and peace of the Lord in their heart because they were not right in their feeling and relationship toward other Christians. "He that loveth his brother abideth in the light, and there is none occasion of stumbling in him." But it goes on, "But he that hateth his brother is in darkness, and walketh in darkness, and knoweth not whither he goeth, because that darkness hath blinded his eyes." A Christian without love is walking in darkness. And God says he doesn't even know where he is going.

We read in I John 3:14, "We know that we have passed from death unto life, because we love the brethren. He that loveth not his brother abideth in death." The Bible teaches the church Jesus built was completely permeated by love.

Paul wrote about the gifts, and there are nine of them. A strange church was this Corinthian church and it was not a perfect church. They had divisions, carnalities, strife, and they were sermon tasters. Some said, "I like this preacher." Others, "I don't care for that one." "I like this one." Paul had to write them about these things. They were not a perfect church. By the way, neither is Emmanuel Baptist Church perfect. If it were, we would never receive you into membership because you would ruin it the day you join it. But the Corinthian church had all nine gifts of the Spirit. People were talking about the gifts. Some said, "The gift of faith is greater than the gift of government." Others said, "And the gift of healing is greater than the gift of tongues." Paul said, in speaking of the gifts, "But covet earnestly the best gifts: and yet shew I unto you a more excellent way" (I Cor. 12:31). And he talked in chapter 13 about love being the greatest of them all.

I care not how talented you are, or how brilliant you are, or how personable you are, or how knowledgeable you are: if you are a Christian, love people! This church Jesus built was a loving church.

First, there ought to be a love for Jesus that surpasses all earthly love. Christians will do things for Jesus they would not do for anybody else. Christians ought to love Jesus supremely. And their love for Him should excel every earthly tie.

A little girl loved Jesus. Her father was an unbeliever. She said to her father one time, "Daddy, do you love Jesus?"

He said, "I have never seen Jesus. He came two thousand years ago and they say He died, and that's the end of Him. And you can't love someone you haven't seen."

This was a smart little girl and she loved the Lord. She said, "Daddy, how old was I when my mother died?"

He said, "You were not even six months old, my dear, when your mother left this world."

She said, "Daddy, I want to tell you something. I love my mother, though I have never seen her. I do not remember touching her as a little baby. I have no idea in the world what she looked like. But I have heard others tell how much she loved me. Others say what a great mother she was. Daddy, I love my mother though I have no recollection of ever seeing her."

And I say to you tonight, like Peter said, "Whom having not seen, ye love" (I Pet. 1:8). Yes, a Christian ought to have a supreme love for Jesus that motivates, directs and changes his life.

The early church was characterized by a love for each other, love for Jesus, love for lost souls. Whenever you find a church that does not have that kind of love, it's not a New Testament, Bible-believing church modeling itself after the church Jesus built.

5. It Was an Obedient Church

In the next place the church Jesus built was an obedient church. As you study about this church, you will see how they got the work done. They won people by the thousands until even their enemies said, "You have filled this city with your teaching" (Jerusalem).

But this church was an obedient church. Now you see them put to test and tempted, as it were, to depart from the Word of God. For instance, we read in Acts 5:29, "Then Peter and the other apostles answered and said, We ought to obey God rather than men." Now why did they say that? Because after that lame man got healed in chapter 3, they got put in jail in chapter 4. Finally twice their enemy said, "Now speak no more in the name of Jesus. We command you not to mention Jesus Christ again." You know what they said? "We ought to obey God rather than men."

So should you. So should I. So should this church. This church will not take orders from some religious denomination. "We ought to obey God rather than men." Great scholars say that the word "ought" could be translated "must." "We must obey God rather than men." So the church Jesus built was an obedient church.

In Acts 5:32 you read, "And we are his witnesses of these things; and so is also the Holy Ghost, whom God hath given to them that obey him." I have heard preachers preach for thirty-eight years on how to be filled with the Holy Spirit. But I have heard only one preacher—one in thirty-eight years—mention the requirement for the filling of the Holy Ghost that the Bible mentions, and that is obedience. I have heard them say, "You have to wait on God." I have heard them say, "You have to empty yourself." But only one preacher in thirty-eight years has ever said, "To have the fullness of the Holy Ghost, you must be an obedient Christian." You can't disobey God, then expect Him to fill you with the Holy Ghost.

Now listen to what it says: "And we are his witnesses of these things; and so is also the Holy Ghost, whom God hath given to them that obey him." Christian, when you disobey God, you cannot be filled with the Holy Spirit.

I was preaching at Grace Theological Seminary years ago for a week. There was a great Bible preacher there, Dr. A. W. Tozer. He went to be with the Lord a few years ago. I was sitting at the table with him one morning. I never asked him about this but he said, "Tom, if a preacher or a Christian is to be filled with the Holy Spirit and have God's power, they are going to have to obey God." I had never thought of it before. Obedience is a requirement for the filling of the Holy Spirit.

This was an obedient church. They said, "You can threaten us not to speak again in the name of Jesus, but we will anyhow because God hath commanded us and, We ought to obey God rather than men."

We get to Acts 6:7: "And the word of God increased; and the number of the disciples multiplied in Jerusalem greatly; and a great company of the priests were obedient to the faith." Now this church obeyed God.

There are so many illustrations in the Bible. I think of Saul of the Old Testament. The first king was really a strange fellow, and a great big fellow. The Bible says he stood head and shoulders above all others. He probably was seven and one-half feet tall.

And if he stood head and shoulders above all of his fellows, he no doubt was an unusually big man. And when the Lord designated him to Samuel as king, he was timid.

This great big old timid fellow would stand around with his head hanging down. But he got to be king and because he was a mighty man, he was successful in war and a few other things.

One day he said, "Now, you know because I'm the king I can do anything I want to do. Others may have to go by rules and regulations, but not me." Samuel the prophet said, "When you go to fight against the Amalekites, slay those people. Bring not beast nor a man back as a result of this." Amalekites were a type of flesh in the Bible. God said, "I want them obliterated, done away with."

Pride got a hold of him. Saul got to thinking, *Now Saul, you would really look great if you would put a chain around old Agag's neck (the king of the Amalekites) and bring him back. And look at all those fat sheep! Wouldn't it be a shame to kill all of those? You know the Lord uses sheep as an animal of sacrifice in the Temple worship. Why, I would hate to kill all of those.* But a still small voice said, "But God said to slay man, woman, the Amalekites. Destroy them. Do what I tell you to do. God does not need anything that the Amalekites have."

But he took those sheep and came back. Samuel met him and said, "Hast thou obeyed the Lord?" About that time out here a little sheep went Bah! Bah! And Samuel said, "What meaneth then this bleating of the sheep?" Saul said, "I thought it would be good to bring them back to offer to God." Samuel said, "To obey is better than sacrifice."

To obey is the greatest thing in the world. And there is a principle here that the Christians of this generation face in just as realistic a way as the Christians in Bible times faced. We must obey God.

I will never forget a crisis in my ministry in this city. Twenty-nine years ago I sat in the ministerial association of this city one day and a discussion was started and began to develop about this subject: Does one have to believe in the virgin birth of Jesus Christ in order to be a Christian? More than fifty ministers in that ministerial association were almost equally divided. Twenty-five said, "You do not have to believe in the virgin birth of Jesus Christ in order to be a Christian." Twenty-five said, "Yes, you do." There they were—equally divided.

That day God seemed to say to me, "Tom, this is no place for a Bible believer. If you are going to obey God and walk with God, you can't walk in a mixed multitude."

I walked out of that big downtown church that day and made a covenant with God. It has cost me some tears, criticism, loss of friends; but listen! We cannot compromise! God says that obedience is better than even worship. This New Testament church was characterized by a spirit of obedience to the Lord and to His Word. Think tonight: Are you obeying the Lord?

6. It Was a Missionary Church

It was a missionary church. Jesus said, "...upon this rock I will build my church." I am not talking about religious groups, nor about denominations; I'm talking about the kind of a church Jesus built and described in the Bible. It was a missionary church.

In Acts 1:8: "But ye shall receive power, after that the Holy Ghost is come upon you: and ye shall be witnesses unto me both in Jerusalem, and in all Judaea, and in Samaria, and unto the uttermost part of the earth."

I want you to see something I believe the Lord showed me out of this verse. People say this verse tells you that you receive power from the Holy Spirit of God to be a witness for the Lord. That is true. And to be a soul winner, and nothing could be any truer than that. But you read in this chapter where the disciples said to Jesus, "Wilt thou at this time restore again the kingdom to Israel?" Jesus said, "It is not for you to know the times or the seasons, which the Father hath put in his own power...." "But wait for the promise," Jesus said. These disciples said, "Rome rules the world. We don't have our own kingdom and we want to have. We want the Jews to have the land and we want our kingdom. Wilt thou at this time restore again the kingdom to Israel? Will you take it out of the hands of the Romans and put it back in the hands of the elect people of God?" Jesus said, "It is not for you to know when God is going to do this." That will take place when the Lord comes again.

Then He went on to say, "But ye shall receive power, after that the Holy Ghost is come upon you; and ye shall be witnesses unto me...." Sometimes even the best Christians put a period right there, but God doesn't. "...ye shall be witnesses unto me both in Jerusalem, and in all Judaea, and in Samaria, and unto the uttermost part of the earth."

God in this verse is giving the church power to be a missionary church. Not just to win people to Christ in their own locality, "But...both in Jerusalem, and in all Judaea, and in Samaria, and unto the uttermost part of the earth." Right in that verse God was saying, "My church is to be a missionary church."

I feel sorry for these people who do not love people of another race. I feel sorry for these people who could not care less about the poor, benighted lost souls across the ocean. God cares! God so loved the world that He gave His only begotten Son. And right here God is saying, "I want my church to be a missionary church."

Now they set out to evangelize their city. Their enemies said, "You have filled this city with your teaching." But they didn't do what Jesus told them to do—not like they should have. The Lord said, "...ye shall be witnesses unto me both in Jerusalem, and in all Judaea, and in Samaria, and unto the uttermost part of the earth.'' The Lord said they were to go to all the known world. They didn't do that.

Come to chapter 6. They elected a board of deacons. Come to chapter 7. One of those deacons preaches a tremendous sermon, Stephen. And they rushed upon Stephen. Gnashing their teeth, they took stones and knocked his brains out. They killed him and dragged him through what is called even today Stephen's Gate.

God had to let one of the deacons be killed. Why? They wouldn't move out. Oh yes, they evangelized Jerusalem, but in chapter 8 we read, ''And Saul was consenting unto his death [Stephen's]. And at that time there was great persecution against the church which was at Jerusalem [They hadn't moved out.]; and they were all scattered abroad throughout the regions of Judaea and Samaria, except the apostles.''

God wanted a missionary church. ''Oh, but we evangelized the city.'' God said, ''What about Judaea? What about Samaria? What about the uttermost parts of the earth?'' Philip, a deacon, went to Samaria after this. I don't blame him. If I had seen Stephen with his brains knocked out and blood flowing from his body, seen them gnash upon him with their teeth and kill him, the Lord wouldn't have had to say twice to me, ''Tom, you had better go to Samaria.'' I would have said, ''Lord, here am I, send me. Which gate do I go out?''

And that's why Philip went to Samaria. Stephen had been killed because the church had not done what God said do in Acts chapter 1 and verse 8.

When Philip went to Samaria, the Ethiopian eunuch got saved and took the Gospel down into the continent of Africa.

Chapter 13 of the Book of Acts is the record of the great church at Antioch which began to send the Gospel to the uttermost parts of the earth. You find for the first time men crossed the waters,

Paul crossed the sea and took the Gospel into Macedonia and later into what is now Asia.

God wants a missionary church. The Lord wants the church to have a well-rounded program of saving people, winning people at home and sending the Gospel to the ends of the earth.

The church that Jesus built was a missionary church.

7. It Was a Persecuted Church

I close by saying that the church Jesus built was a persecuted and a hated church. You say that was back when people were not civilized. That's back when people didn't know any better. No; that was back when Christians lived like the Bible says live. That's why they were hated. That's why they were persecuted.

You read of this persecution in Acts 4:1, 2:

"And as they spake unto the people, the priests, and the captain of the temple, and the Sadducees, came upon them [persecution will come from religious people], *Being grieved that they taught the people, and preached through Jesus the resurrection from the dead."*

It was a persecuted church.

And in Acts 4:17, "But that it spread no further among the people, let us straitly threaten them, that they speak henceforth to no man in this name." When did that take place? After they got that fellow healed at the Gate Beautiful. He was forty years old. Thousands had passed him by. He had held up his tin cup and begged for pennies, but nobody had done anything for him.

One day Peter and John came by and he asked them for some money. Peter said, "Silver and gold have I none; but such as I have give I thee: In the name of Jesus Christ of Nazareth rise up and walk." Peter took him by the hand and "his feet and ankle bones received strength. And he leaping up stood...."

Then they were put in jail and kept there all night. The next morning the Sanhedrin brought them out, put them in the middle of them and began to question them. I can see these old Pharisees stroking their long beards and one of them saying, "Now, one thing you can't deny and that is, a notable miracle has been wrought here. He sat at that gate, a forty-year-old man. He ought to know whether he was healed or not. Nobody else ever did anything. They saw a man who was a cripple, now he is well." The spokesman said, "This we cannot deny."

When I read that I get encouraged and think, *Maybe they are going to see things our way.* But they didn't. "You can't deny that a miracle has been wrought. And all the people know it. But threaten them. Tell them not to speak any more in the name of Jesus." And then I read these words, "So when they had further threatened them, they let them go" (Acts 4:21). They said, "We know they are right. We know that they got a man saved. We know that a miracle has been wrought, but threaten them anyway."

If you think that this world is a friend of a born-again child of God, you have another thought coming.

Persecution in Bible times only came when Christians witnessed. It was not while they were praying, singing, or going to the house of God; they were persecuted when they witnessed for Jesus Christ!

A man told me the other day that he was in the airport at Washington, D. C., giving out tracts. A policeman came up and said, "Let me see what you have there." He handed him one and he looked at it. Handing it back, he said, "Don't give out any more of those in here."

The man said, "But this is the Word of God."

"I know, but don't give out any more of those in here."

He said, "Is it against the law?"

"If you don't want me to apprehend you, don't give that out in here."

The man said, "Policeman, you take one. You need to be saved."

"No, I don't want one. And don't let me catch you giving out another pamphlet in this airport. If you do, I'll take and book you and put you in jail."

That's the capital of America! If you think God can bless that kind of a nation, you've another thought coming. If you think this world is a friend of a born-again Christian, you have another thought coming. This world hates witnessing people. Jesus said, "They will hate you because they hated Me." I would rather they love me. But the church Jesus built was with Christians who set out to win people to the Lord and were hated by the ungodly.

". . .upon this rock I will build my church; and the gates of hell shall not prevail against it." —Matt. 16:18.

Chapter XV

The Signs of a Dead Church

(Preached at the Emmanuel Baptist Church in Pontiac, Michigan, 1963)

READ: Revelation 3:1-6

"...I know thy works, that thou hast a name that thou livest, and art dead."—Rev. 3:1.

Jesus said this to a New Testament church. I do not know that anyone in the world could tell you why the church at Sardis was looked upon as a dead church. I do know that when I read the message Jesus sent to it, I find this church had no persecution. That might have been one reason why it died. To make no enemies, to have no one against it, to never have persecution, is one of the surest ways to kill a church. I don't know whether that is what killed this one, but the church at Sardis suffered no persecution. It had no opposition. It endured no hardships This church had it easy. That may be the explanation of why it died.

Jesus said, "You have a name that you live, but you are not really alive; you are a dead church."

Several things are said in the New Testament about the condition of churches and individuals. While I am speaking on the signs of a dead church, if you will be honest and will give God your attention, you will not only know why a church is dead, but you will know why Christians are dead. And you may even want to ask yourself, "Am I dead?"

Jesus made this statement in Matthew 13:25, "But while men slept, his enemy came and sowed tares among the wheat, and went his way."

Who are those "men"? Without any shadow of doubt, they were God's men, Christians, the light of the world, the salt of the earth. Jesus said that they "slept" when they should have been awake. That is indictment enough for God to say His church is asleep, when it ought to be awake. But this is a lot worse here. Jesus said, "You are not just asleep; you are dead. Not only that, you have a name, a testimony that you live, when the truth is, you are a dead church."

That is what He wrote to the church at Sardis.

Now if you think it impossible to have a name that you live and at the same time, be dead, I will show you another verse—I Timothy 5:6: "But she that liveth in pleasure is dead while she liveth." God said that you can be dead even while you are living. Paradoxical though it may sound, yet it is possible for a church to have a name that it lives, but to be a church that is dead.

I am sorry to say that I have known such churches. I have heard, ever since I have been a Christian, about a great church in Atlanta, Georgia, and read about some of its pastors. For about forty years one man was looked upon as one of the greatest leaders this country has known. As a Christian, a young man, I could not wait for the opportunity to view that church in Atlanta.

I went to Atlanta some years ago to preach. I asked some folks, "What about such and such a church? Is it still the great church that it used to be, when souls were saved, when great victories came, when God was working miracles in that place?"

They shook their heads and said, "No, that church is no longer a live church."

I thought of one great man who gave nearly four decades of his life to the ministry of that church and saw literally hundreds and thousands saved. When they said, "It is no longer a live church," I wondered, from the depth of my heart, what killed that church.

I could multiply that story. I could take you to the great city of Boston, and I could show you a church where the great preachers of generations past have preached and great multitudes came and hundreds were saved. Some of the greatest revivals ever held in America were held there.

But it is no longer that kind of a church. A cold, theological, technical technician preaches professionally in the pulpit. There are no altar calls, no revivals, no warmth, no friendliness It is a dead church. But it used to be very much alive.

I could take you to New York City. I could name a great Baptist church; the names of its pastors have gone down in history as God-fearing gospel preachers. Now that church is dead. No longer is it a living church.

There are two ways you can approach it. You can have an examination while you are living, or have an autopsy after you are dead. We might as well make up our minds which we want. Physically speaking, you go to the doctor and get an examination. The doctor tells you what is wrong with you. If you have good sense, you will get it taken care of. If you haven't, before long they will say to your wife or some member of your family, "Would you sign this paper giving permission to perform an autopsy to see what killed your loved one?"

That is the way it will happen. You can either have an examination, or you can have the possibility of an autopsy. I wish this would not be an autopsy but a spiritual examination. These are the signs of a dead church, or what kills churches.

And the same thing that kills churches kills Christians. The same thing that rocks churches to sleep, rocks individual Christians to sleep.

Now what are the signs? If you and I are as sincere as we claim to be, and if we mean business with God and with others as we say that we do, we will face these things. Where God speaks, we will listen. Where the sharp arrows of God's Word sting our souls, we will make adjustment. While the white searchlight of God's Holy Ghost makes an examination, we will make the corrections. God has a remedy for coldness and deadness.

What are the signs of a dead church, though it may have a name that lives? There is no question but that this church—Emmanuel Baptist Church—has a name that lives. I say that humbly and with fear and trembling. The name of this church has gone around the world. This is a church out of whose doors have poured a constant stream of young men and women going to the mission fields and to pulpits to preach the Gospel. This is a church whose ministry has seen people saved, either by the printed page or through missionaries or preachers all around the globe, in nearly every country in all the world. In every state in the union, this is a church that lives.

But is it living? That is what I am asking you. God says you can have a name that you are living, yet be dead.

I. WHEN THERE IS NO BURDEN FOR SOULS

When there is no burden for souls—a longing, a thirsting, a hungering, an all-absorbing burning passion that there constantly be people saved in the church—then that means a church is either dead or dying.

I would to God that we could have a burden even close to what Paul had. He said in Romans 9:1-3:

"I say the truth in Christ, I lie not, my conscience also bearing me witness in the Holy Ghost, That I have great heaviness and

continual sorrow in my heart. For I could wish that my self were accursed from Christ for my brethren, my kinsmen according to the flesh. "

Paul said, "The Holy Ghost and my conscience must bear witness together that there is a longing in my heart to see people saved."

I believe we have members of Emmanuel Baptist Church who, if a soul were never saved from this night on, would never lose a moment's sleep or shed a tear.

Friends, we need a burden for souls! Preachers need it. Church members need it. No burden is a sign that a church is either dead or dying. We have no other manual but the Bible. We have no headquarters from where we get literature. We go by the Book of God! Psalm 126:5 says, "They that sow in tears shall reap in joy." If there is not sowing in tears, then if this Bible be true, there is no reaping in joy. God said it: "They that sow in tears shall reap in joy."

You say to me, "Why is there not more reaping in joy?" I say to you, "Because there is no sowing in tears."

Some Christians in this generation have too much pride to weep. I have watched them. I have seen them fight back the tears: it would be a disgrace for them to weep in public. God says in Psalm 126:6, "He that goeth forth AND WEEPETH, bearing precious seed, shall doubtless come again with rejoicing, bringing his sheaves with him." According to this verse, it is not enough just to go. I believe in the "going." I would to God that we had ten times more people going. God said, "He that goeth forth . . ."; but He doesn't stop there: ". . . and WEEPETH, bearing precious seed, shall doubtless come again with rejoicing, bringing his sheaves with him."

You say, "Where is the coming again? Where is the bringing in the sheaves?" I say to you, "Where is the going forth and the weeping?"

We have too many dry-eyed Christians. There have been times when I have preached with no tears. But God's Word teaches that there must be a burden for lost souls. I leave it right there. It is between the Book and you, between God and you. Where there is no burden for souls, a church is either dead or dying.

"Thou hast a name that thou livest, and art dead."

II. WHEN THERE IS NO HUNGER FOR THE WORD OF GOD

When there is no hunger for the Word of God, the church is either dead or dying. One of the most wonderful things about the Bible is what it says about itself. In many ways, the 119th Psalm is the greatest piece of literature ever written. There are twenty-two letters in the Hebrew alphabet. There are twenty-two stanzas in the 119th Psalm, and eight verses in each stanza. From Aleph to Tau in the Hebrew alphabet, every one of these twenty-two stanzas begins with a different letter of the Hebrew alphabet. No poet ever wrote anything like it. No literary genius ever wrote anything to compare to it. It has ten different names for the Bible: the Way, the Word, the Testimonies, the Law, the Precepts, the Statutes, the Judgments, the Commandments, etc. And in the midst of it, verse 103 says, "How sweet are thy words unto my taste! yea, sweeter than honey to my mouth!"

Where now are the Christians who have a hunger, a longing for the Bible and its preaching, those who long for the Lord's Day to come so they can hear the Word of God?

Verse 11 says, "Thy word have I hid in mine heart, that I might not sin against thee." Where are the Christians who are constantly hiding the Word of God in their hearts? First Peter 2:2 says, "As newborn babes, desire the sincere milk of the word, that ye may grow thereby." I ask you, where are the Christians who desire, who hunger, who thirst, who long for the Word of God?

The Word of God is living. Listen to Hebrews 4:12: "For the word of God is quick, and powerful, and sharper than any two-edged sword, piercing even to the dividing asunder of soul and spirit, and of the joints and marrow, and is a discerner of the thoughts and intents of the heart." God says that this Word is LIVING.

I love it—and it loves me back. I press it—and it oozes blood. I listen to it—and I hear it breathe. This Book is a living Book. Oh, a church that has no hunger for the Word of God is either dead or dying!

We need, once again, to put this old Book where it belongs. The church is not a club, but a place where God's Word is preached. The church is not a business, but a place where God's Word is honored. It not only ought to have first place; it ought to have the only place! Everything is subservient to it. Everything is to exalt it. Every song is to exalt the Christ of this Bible. A church has no right to exist when it does not major in the preaching of the Word of God. When there is no hunger for the Word of God, the church is either dead or dying. And remember what I said to you about the signs of a dead church being the signs of a dead Christian.

III. WHEN THERE IS NO HUNGER FOR CHRISTIAN FELLOWSHIP

Hebrews 10:25 says, "Not forsaking the assembling of ourselves together, as the manner of some is; but exhorting one another: and so much the more, as ye see the day approaching." God exhorts us not to ever forsake the assembling of ourselves together, for Christian fellowship centers around the person of the Lord Jesus and together, as a living body or organism. So when there is no hunger for fellowship, the Christian is dead or dying.

If you can be satisfied to never meet with the people of God, only fellowship with those of the world, then you may need to be born again. It is hardly possible to be a Christian and not want Christian fellowship. Jesus said, ''Where two or three are gathered together in my name, there will I be in the midst.'' That is what fellowship is. Oh, when you have no hunger for Christian fellowship, then you are a dead Christian—I John 1:7: ''But if we walk in the light, as he is in the light, we have fellowship one with another, and the blood of Jesus Christ his Son cleanseth us from all sin.''

A lot of folks who are out of sorts cannot live in that verse. I say it with pity and tenderness: many a Christian in this old world is so out of sorts that he cannot live in that verse. First Corinthians 11:17 says, ''Now in this that I declare unto you I praise you not, that ye come together not for the better, but for the worse.''

A lot of churches are meeting without fellowship. God's holy Book says that their coming together is not for the best but for the worst. They would be better off not to meet than to meet and not meet right.

We need fellowship. Call it what you want to. God says, 'If a man say that he loves God whom he hath not seen and hates his brother, he is a liar.' How can he love God whom he hath not seen, and hate his brother whom he hath seen? I think I know what that means. Every saved man and woman in this church is a picture of God. Don't you say that I said we have some deity in us! Not one of us is worth the snap of my finger as far as having any righteousness of our own. As far as the flesh is concerned, I don't trust you, and I don't trust myself. I have no confidence in your flesh or mine. But we are born again, and there has been imparted unto us a new nature. Someone came to live in our body. We are the temple of God and a picture of God. We are made in His image, indwelt by His presence, washed in His blood, held in His hand and loved in His heart. If we cannot fellowship together, then we cannot fellowship with our brothers and sisters, and we cannot have fellowship with God.

We need fellowship. We need a warmth and a friendliness. Our very looks tell what kind of a Christian we are. The way some of you look is a disgrace! You look like you just lost your job. I think I'll get me some blinders if I keep preaching to you! I can't see anything but the Bible with blinders on! Now a smile from you will help me. My stars! You are beautiful when you smile! If you have no teeth, smile anyway! Show your gums! Anything looks better than that frown.

We need warmth. The very look on the faces of most modern Christians tells a lost and needy world, "My problems are bigger than God." The look on our faces ought to say to the whole wide world, "My God is bigger than my sins, my problems, my failures." We need warmth.

We used to talk about southern hospitality. I know you Yankees won't get mad at me, because we are still fighting the Civil War. It has never ended. I guess we could never draw up any terms, because it is still going on. We used to talk about "southern hospitality." In many instances, there is no such thing. Some of the meanest, prune-faced people I have ever met in my life, I met below the Mason-Dixon Line. But there used to be a southern hospitality, when you could visit the old-fashioned neighbors who, when they said, "Stay all night with me," meant it. When you started to leave, even if you had stayed all day, they would say, "What's your hurry?" Each delighted in his humble home and simple food. All had the old-fashioned water bucket, and everyone drank out of the same dipper. They knew the meaning of love and fellowship.

You would get ready to go home, and they would say, "Stay for supper."

"No, I'd better go."

"No, come on and eat with us."

There was a warmth there. I have stayed all night with such folk. They would throw an old quilt down on the floor and say, "There's your bed." We call them pallets.

In our churches we need warmth and Christian fellowship.

"Thou hast a name that thou livest, and art dead."

IV. WHEN THERE IS NO LIBERTY OF THE HOLY GHOST

We read in II Corinthians 3:17, "Now the Lord is that Spirit: and where the Spirit of the Lord is, there is liberty." A church where the Holy Spirit has no liberty is like a wheel on an axle with no grease. It grinds and makes an awful noise. We must have the Holy Ghost in our church. We must have His power and His blessing. We must have the liberty of the Holy Spirit.

We must never let ritual grieve Him. I never saw such a ritual-minded generation in my life. A lot of people start churches and call them independent, fundamental, Bible-believing churches; yet they bury everything in such ritual. The choir comes out with a sevenfold "Hallelujah" that the one who wrote the song couldn't even interpret. The preacher comes out, reads from one pulpit on the left; and the next thing you know, he is at another one on the right, while you are trying to find out where he went! They have to have two pulpits, and neither is in the middle. Half of the time he is standing sideways and looking off yonder but seeing nothing. He has on a black night gown that he forgot to take off when he came to church! A bunch of foolishness! God never meant it that way.

Someone says, "John Wesley wore a robe." Well, if I had what John Wesley had, I could wear one, and heat it up, too! All this ritual is a bunch of foolishness.

Someone says, "Why, don't you have a bulletin?" No, we don't.

We don't want to be bound to an order of service. We may want to have two baptisms instead of one—like we had tonight!

The Holy Spirit of God is grieved by a struggle for prominence. He is grieved when the services are given over to dignity. Some will not come to this church because "we just can't stand loud preaching." The Bible says that Jesus "lifted up his voice." I can't stand to listen to a man who won't speak up. Where in the Bible do you read, "Let us have dignified services"?

The most dignified person I ever met was over in Egypt. Mrs. Malone and I visited the Museum in Cairo, Egypt. King Tut's tomb had been uncovered 450 miles south of there, the richest tomb in the world. King Tut was laid out in three solid gold mummy cases, each one of which was worth twenty million dollars. His coffin cost sixty million dollars, I am told. There is no telling how many precious stones and jewels were buried with him. It has been said that it was the richest funeral ever held in the history of the world.

I met King Tut in that museum. There he was. When I said, "How are you, Tut, old boy?" he never opened his mouth. He never moved a muscle, never flicked an eyelid. I have never met a more dignified gentleman. Only one thing was wrong with him. He was deader than a mackerel.

So if you want dignity, you will have to find it somewhere else. I took a Bible concordance and looked up the word *dignity*. Ecclesiastes 10:6 says, "Folly is set in great dignity, and the rich sit in low place." God says that you can have it if you want it, but it is a bunch of foolishness.

Some churches are trying their best to be dignified and yet still be fundamental, so no one will attend but the elite. You can't do that. A dear man came to me recently and told me that another Baptist church in our city had asked him not to come back because his shirt was wrinkled. We welcome that kind of people here at Emmanuel.

V. WHEN THE JOY OF THE LORD IS GONE

When the joy of the Lord is gone, it is a sign that the church is either dead or dying.

Listen, don't any man or woman ever say, "Amen!" in this church because I think you ought to. Get so happy in God that sometimes you can't help but burst out.

About once a year Grandma Freeland shouts in our church. This sweet old Alabama woman gets happy. There is always something sweet about someone from Alabama! I met a man this morning from Alabama. It was all I could do to keep from hugging him! I am so glad that Grandma Freeland shouts because when I am away someone says, "Does anyone ever get shouting happy in your church?" I am able to say, "Yes—about once a year."

About a month ago, Grandma Freeland clapped her hands and hollered. I sat back and said in my heart, *Go to it, Grandma! Have a good time!* Some of you got strange looks on your faces. Some of you thought she was too loud. I thank God for her happy praise.

When a woman got happy in a certain church, the preacher grabbed his little phone, called the usher and said, "Come down here and tell that woman to shut up."

The usher came down the aisle and said, "Now you will have to quiet down. We don't have that here."

She said, "But I've got religion!"

He said, "Well, you didn't get it here. So, be quiet!"

A lot of places you won't get it.

They got a new theological preacher at this black man's church. And you know, some of those black preachers have lost it, too. Why, I used to hear the colored preachers preach, and they did not have a grammar school education. They would frighten me to death. I heard a colored preacher preach in the red clay hills of Alabama, when I was a boy. He preached on the flood. He said again and again, "It is goin' ta rain. It is goin' ta rain."

I kept looking up. I expected it to rain any minute. Then he told the story of the judgment of God on the world. He had something. I would to God that I could believe that we would never lose that in this church. This old black farmer would get happy. Thinking about being saved and going to Heaven and his family being saved and thinking of his loved ones he was going to meet, he just couldn't be still.

The new theological preacher sent two or three deacons out to the farm to tell him that if he was going to continue making noise and saying, "Amen!" he would have to quit coming to that church.

They went out. He was plowing with one old mule and a single stock plow on the little rock farm. He stopped his mule and they said, "The preacher sent us to tell you that you are making too much fuss in the services. You say, 'Amen!' and, 'Praise the Lord!' You have to stop it."

The old colored guy took his hat off, leaned over on his plow and said, "I am sorry—I really am. I didn't mean to disturb nobody. I sure want to apologize. I wouldn't do anything in the world to hurt the church or cause a burden on my pastor. I am awful sorry. But you know, I get to thinking about how I used to be a drunkard and on my way to Hell, how my family was hungry and needed clothes, and how one day Jesus saved me and I started a new life, started making a living and putting clothes on the backs of my little kids and food in their mouths. My wife is so happy. Some of my little children have gone on to Heaven. I gets to thinking about how someday I'm gonna see 'em in Glory. I gets to thinking that my name is written in the Lamb's Book of Life, and I can almost see Master Jesus up there. Deacons, hold this mule. I'm gonna' shout as sure as the world!"

I wish we had a few like that. Don't ever act the fool. Don't ever do anything you do not feel. But FEEL IT! God knows we need to feel it. We will either feel it or die. One of the signs of a dead church is when the joy of the Lord is gone.

"Thou hast a name that thou livest, and art dead."

VI. WHEN THERE IS NO SPIRIT OF PRAYER

A great man who has won many people to the Lord and built one of the greatest churches there ever has been built—I heard someone say to him, "Preacher, could you name something that had a great bearing on the building of this church?"

This preacher, with all the humility in the world, said, "This church was built on John 14:14, 'If ye shall ask any thing in my name, I will do it.' "

I got to thinking about that. I thought, *Surely that could not be true.* Did he mean that this church was built on nothing but prayer? No, he did not mean that. But he meant that all the visitation, the preaching, the living, the winning, the singing, was saturated in prayer.

God answers prayer. I have seen miracles performed in answer to prayer. As I saw that great group coming this morning here in this church to be saved, I knew God had answered my prayer.

How long has it been since you got down on your knees and prayed, "O God, bless my church. God, help my preacher preach with power. God, save souls in our church"? How long has it been? It is a sign that the Christians and the church are either dead or dying. God says, "Call upon me, and I will answer thee, and shew thee great and mighty things..." (Jer. 33:3).

VII. WHEN THERE IS NO WILLINGNESS TO SERVE WITH SACRIFICE

When you cannot get people to do the hard jobs, when folks will only serve in public jobs, not the hard ones that are done in private, the church is either dead or dying.

My time is up, but remember that Jesus never said it would be easy. "If any man will come after me, let him deny himself and take up his cross daily and follow me" (Luke 9:23). It takes a real, live Christian to go upstream, to keep his face always turned toward the enemy and be willing to suffer for Christ.

"Thou hast a name that thou livest, and art dead." Rev. 3:1.

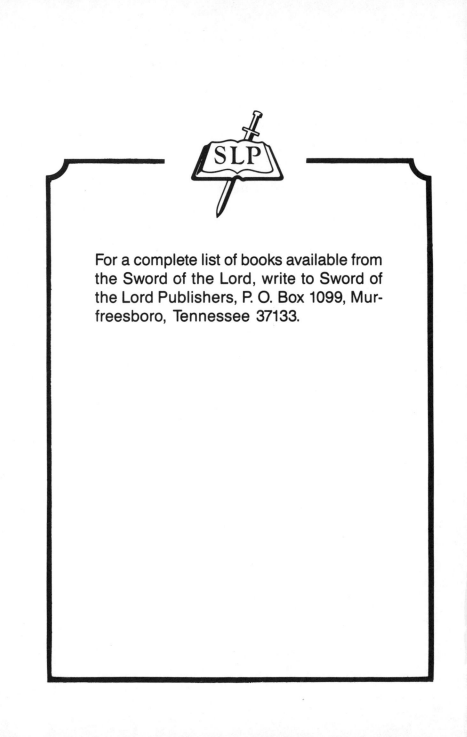

For a complete list of books available from the Sword of the Lord, write to Sword of the Lord Publishers, P. O. Box 1099, Murfreesboro, Tennessee 37133.